MW00635516

Making the
SABBATH
A DELIGHT

OTHER COVENANT BOOKS AND AUDIO BOOKS
BY BRENT L. TOP:

Glimpses beyond Death's Door

Protecting against Eternal Identity Theft

*Of These Emblems: Coming Closer to Christ
through the Sacrament*

Strength through Adversity

Becoming More Christlike

OTHER COVENANT BOOKS AND AUDIO BOOKS
BY BRENT L. TOP AND WENDY C. TOP:

Finding Inner Peace

Making the
SABBATH
A DELIGHT

BRENT L. TOP
AND WENDY C. TOP

Covenant Communications, Inc.

Cover image: *I Shall Not Want* © Yongsung Kim, Used with permission from LightHaven. For print information, go to www.lighthaven.net or call 1-800-366-2781.

Cover design copyright © 2017 by Covenant Communications, Inc.

Published by Covenant Communications, Inc.
American Fork, Utah

Copyright © 2017 by Brent L. Top and Wendy C. Top
All rights reserved. No part of this book may be reproduced in any format or in any medium without the written permission of the publisher, Covenant Communications, Inc., P.O. Box 416, American Fork, UT 84003. This work is not an official publication of The Church of Jesus Christ of Latter-day Saints. The views expressed within this work are the sole responsibility of the author and do not necessarily reflect the position of The Church of Jesus Christ of Latter-day Saints, Covenant Communications, Inc., or any other entity.

Printed in the United States of America
First Printing: April 2017

23 22 21 20 19 18 17 10 9 8 7 6 5 4 3 2 1

ISBN 978-1-52440-248-8

TABLE OF CONTENTS

PREFACE
"Call the Sabbath a Delight"

YOU CAN FEEL THE EXCITEMENT and anticipation in the air on a late Friday afternoon in Jerusalem. Orthodox men and women quicken their pace as they rush in and out of shops and marketplaces to finish their last-minute preparations for the Shabbat that will begin eighteen minutes before sundown. The women purchase their *challah*, the soft, sweet, eggy, braided bread that is made especially for Shabbat. They hurry home to clean their houses and prepare meals that can be eaten on Shabbat without any preparation other than reheating in their specially equipped pre-programmed Sabbath ovens. They bathe themselves and their children and get the family dressed up in time to fulfill the obligation designated to Jewish women—the lighting of the two Shabbat candles that will signify the beginning of their Sabbath observance.

Men likewise have responsibilities. With skull caps on their heads, they scurry down the street from a shortened day at work or a *Yeshiva* (place to study Torah) to catch a bus that will take them home in time to bathe and put on their best clothes to conduct the family's worship. Some trek to synagogue services. Others welcome "Queen Sabbath" by praying and singing at the Western Wall—the remnant of the retaining wall of Herod's Temple compound, the holiest place in Judaism.

Traffic on the otherwise congested and chaotic streets gradually thins out and virtually disappears. Public bus service shuts down. Even as others make their last-minute purchases, shop owners and vendors are in the process of closing down so that they too may hurry home in time to be with their families, the place where Sabbath begins and ends among observant Jews.

Rarely do we as Latter-day Saints speak of "celebrating" the Sabbath, even though that is exactly what the Lord has commanded us to do (see Leviticus 23:32), but that is certainly how we would describe the way the Orthodox Jews view the coming of their Sabbath. One Jewish commentator, Tracey R. Rich, describes it this way:

> People who do not observe Shabbat think of it as a day filled with stifling restrictions, or as a day of prayer like the Christian Sabbath. But to those who observe Shabbat, it is a precious gift from [God], a day of great joy eagerly awaited throughout the week, a time when we can set aside all of our weekday concerns and devote ourselves to higher pursuits. In Jewish literature, poetry and music, Shabbat is described as a bride or queen, as in the popular Shabbat hymn Lecha Dodi Likrat Kallah (come, my beloved, to meet the [Sabbath] bride). It is said "more than Israel has kept Shabbat, Shabbat has kept Israel."[1]

Wow! Are we missing something? That was the question we had to ask ourselves as we witnessed the celebration of the Sabbath in Jerusalem and in many other cities throughout Israel. We were especially moved by the literal celebrating at the Western Wall when our family lived in Israel in 1994. Late one Friday afternoon, we made our way through the old walled city of Jerusalem to the Jewish Quarter to witness the weekly spectacle. Joy and excitement rippled through the spacious plaza between the Jewish Quarter and the Western Wall as sundown approached.

As worshippers and tourists poured into the open area from the *souk* (covered markets) of the Old City, a large formation of *Yeshiva* students quickstepped their way in perfect unison across the plaza singing a cheery, chanty welcome to the Sabbath as they went. It was all we could do to keep from joining them! On reaching the enclosure in front of the Wall, they covered their heads with their prayer shawls and crowded up next to the ancient stone wall to pray. Rocking back

---

[1] www.jewfaq.org/shabbat.htm

and forth, they worshipped with their whole bodies and souls. Men and women on their respective sides of the enclosure were singing and dancing in undulating lines and circles. Huge Torah scrolls in their ornate cases were marched out in joyous procession and read with great enthusiasm by rabbis. We felt overwhelmed at their devotion and deeply humbled as we realized that perhaps we did not welcome or observe our own Sabbath day with such enthusiasm and devotion. We felt that we as Latter-day Saints could certainly improve our worship, appreciation, and perhaps even adoration of the Sabbath day.

We are not suggesting that Latter-day Saints should sing and dance their way into the Sabbath, but we are saying that we may have a lot to learn from Orthodox Jews about our attitude and observance of that singular day. To paraphrase a trite but true phrase, the Sabbath is a holy gift from God to us, and what we do with it is our gift to God. Our Father in Heaven did not command that we devote one day out of seven to Him because He is vain and demanding. Quite the opposite. "The Sabbath was made for man" (Mark 2:27), the Lord explained in His earthly ministry—made to bless and benefit him, made to rest and sanctify him, made to beckon him back to eternal life in the presence of God. Yet, "what doth it profit a man if a gift is bestowed upon him, and he receive not the gift? Behold, he rejoices not in that which is given unto him, neither rejoices in him who is the giver of the gift" (D&C 88:33). Imagine the blessings awaiting us as individuals, families, communities, and as a church as we open our eyes to the true grandeur of the Sabbath of our Lord, as we enrich our Sabbath worship and devotion, as we fully embrace the joyous gift and opportunity of a day to focus on being as much like God as possible. If the keeping of Shabbat has kept Israel (the Jews) for almost six thousand years, think what it can do for the Latter-day Saints.

Now and then, in our feeble efforts to hallow the Sabbath, we have caught a glimpse of the heavenly blessings of keeping the fourth commandment. We hope to share here some of the insights into the meaning of this commandment that we have gained from our time in Israel, from the holy scriptures, from prophets and apostles, and from trial and error in our own lives. We certainly don't have it perfected.

It is a lifetime process. We just hope that over time, as in all of our efforts to follow Christ, we get a little better as we go. As you read this book with your mind open to impressions of the Spirit that will help you improve your own Sabbath observance and worship, keep in mind that, as with all of our efforts, "the Lord looketh on the heart" (1 Samuel 16:7).

In April 2015, the First Presidency and Quorum of the Twelve Apostles introduced a renewed emphasis on proper observance of the Sabbath day. They provided training to General Authorities, General Auxiliary leaders, Area Seventies, and local leaders. They, in turn, taught this prophetic priority in stake conferences, ward councils, and other settings. Elder M. Russell Ballard, in speaking to the General Officers of the Church at the April 2015 General Conference Leadership Training meeting, declared:

> Of all the organizational or policy changes or doctrinal training that could hasten the work of salvation at this time, we [the First Presidency and Quorum of the Twelve Apostles] have determined that *elevating the spirit and power of the Sabbath day would be most influential in drawing members and families to the Lord Jesus Christ.*[2]

As stated by the Brethren, the primary objective of this training was to build faith in Heavenly Father and the Lord Jesus Christ and His Atonement through Sabbath observance. With increased faith, deeper conversion to the Lord and His Church could be expected. This renewed emphasis by the Lord's prophets, seers, and revelators came, as Elder D. Todd Christofferson explained, "after sustained discussions in the Quorum of the Twelve with the First Presidency about how to strengthen the Church." He said,

> In a natural revelatory process the Lord made known His wish that His ancient commandment regarding the Sabbath, or as the scriptures describe it,

---

[2] M. Russell Ballard, General Conference Leadership Training, April 2015; www.lds.org/broadcasts/archive/general-conference-leadership-training/2015/04?lang=eng; see also *Church News,* July 15, 2015.

"His perpetual covenant with His people," be brought to the fore.

We realize that a deeper understanding of the meaning and purposes of the Sabbath day would bring to the Latter-day Saints a more profound faith in God and in His Son Jesus Christ and the Atonement of Christ. This would build strength in the members of the Church far greater than could be achieved by any programmatic means. We saw that observing the Sabbath could lead to full conversion and spiritual resilience in the Saints. In particular, we came to recognize more fully the importance of the ordinance of the sacrament.[3]

We were inspired and motivated by this renewed emphasis and the training. From that came our desire to contribute to the discussion and, in our small way, add our witness to those of the Brethren. Such was the impetus for this book. In that context, we have two main objectives guiding our writing of this book—1) to provide a general historical and scriptural overview of the Sabbath through different dispensations of the gospel, and 2) to teach the doctrine of the Sabbath from the standard works and teachings of latter-day prophets and apostles, and from those teachings draw applications to our own lives and circumstances as we seek to honor and be blessed by Sabbath observance. The Sabbath truly is His day—a day that is different from all others, sacred and significant in what it represents and what it has to offer to us.

This book is organized according to those two primary purposes. The first part addresses the why and how of Sabbath worship in Old Testament times, Jesus's examples and teachings concerning Sabbath worship found in the New Testament, the transition from Saturday (Shabbat) to Sunday worship (the Lord's day) in early Christianity, and what the Lord has revealed in the dispensation of the fulness of times through the Prophet Joseph Smith. This background

[3] D. Todd Christofferson, General Conference Leadership Training, October 2015; www.lds.org/broadcasts/archive/general-conference-leadership-training/2015/10?lang=eng.

information—historical and scriptural—gives context and perspective to the last part of the book, where we seek to teach what the doctrine of the Sabbath means to us today. It is our hope that what we present in this book both *informs* and *inspires*. More important than just knowing the history, culture, or doctrinal development of Sabbath is the deeply personal knowledge of the meaning and promised blessings of reverencing the Lord's day. That was our intent as we wrote this book, and it is our hope for you as you read it.

We do not profess to be "Sabbath day scholars"—experts in ancient history and culture—nor are we "experts" on living the Sabbath in our own lives, even though we are trying to do better in honoring the Lord on His holy day. In no way are we, by writing this book, holding ourselves up as authorities or examples. However, we seek to share with you some of the insights we have gained from study and experience that may enrich your understanding of and love for the Lord's day. We express appreciation to many who have taught us about the true meaning of the Sabbath, often without even knowing they were teaching us. Their insights and examples have blessed us and we hope we can in small measure pay it forward.

The ideas and applications presented in this book do not represent the official doctrine or position of The Church of Jesus Christ of Latter-day Saints, nor would we want anyone to assume that we are speaking for the leadership of the Church. We recognize that doctrine in the Church is only declared by the Lord's anointed prophets, seers, and revelators. We sustain them wholeheartedly. We have tried our best to ensure that the insights and teachings contained in this book are in harmony with the standard works and teachings of the leaders of the Church. If there are doctrinal deficiencies, they come from our own weaknesses. It is our fervent hope that the Spirit will bear witness to you of the truth and inspire you in your Sabbath worship, and that, in turn, your faith and family will be strengthened.

CHAPTER 1
Holy Envy

RECENTLY ONE OF BRENT'S COLLEAGUES at BYU visited Israel. It was his very first time in the Holy Land. We were particularly interested to hear about his experience, because we have been there many times and we have a deep love for the places and peoples of that place. It so happened that he was in Jerusalem for both the Jewish celebration of Passover and the Christian commemoration of Easter. He told us that he was overwhelmed by the expressions of religious devotion that he witnessed among the people, whether they be Jews, Christians, or Muslims.

We know exactly what he was talking about. We have been to those spiritual sites many times and have observed devout worshippers there expressing their deep religious feelings in their own unique ways—ways that may strike a Latter-day Saint as strange. Yet we are always touched by their obvious dedication to God. Our faith in humanity is strengthened as we witness their adoration for God. What we have in common as children of the same God—and what we can learn from each other about worshipping Him—may be more significant than most of the cultural or doctrinal differences we may have.

The late Krister Stendahl, who served as Lutheran bishop of Stockholm, Sweden, and later as a professor and dean of the Harvard Divinity School, was a noted champion for religious understanding among all of God's children. Amidst vocal opposition to the building of the Stockholm LDS temple, Stendahl came to the defense of the Church. To the critics, he proposed "Three Rules of Religious Understanding":

1. When you are trying to understand another religion, you should seek information from the adherents of that religion and not its enemies.

2. Don't compare your best to their worst.

3. Leave room for "holy envy." By this, Stendahl meant that you should be willing to recognize elements in other religious traditions or faith that you admire and wish could in some way be reflected in your own faith or religious practice.

We have experienced this kind of "holy envy" many times as we have observed and interacted with people of other faith traditions. We'd like to share one example that strengthened our desire to live our own religion and more sincerely worship the Lord.

We first became acquainted with Rabbi David Rosen while Brent was teaching at the BYU Jerusalem Center. Rabbi Rosen taught classes on Judaism and Jewish history. We gained a great appreciation for him not only as a teacher, but also for his personal faith and devotion. Each semester David brought his family to the center to celebrate a Jewish Sabbath with the students and faculty. We became his "family" for that Shabbat.

While it was designed to be a cultural and educational experience for the BYU students, it became a powerful, life-changing experience for us. As we sang traditional Jewish Sabbath songs at the Shabbat meal, we could see the utter joy and delight on Rabbi Rosen's face. He and his family actually enjoyed the Sabbath—they loved being together, singing together, eating together, talking of spiritual things together, and most of all showing their love for God together. There were no complaints of what they couldn't do—and as Orthodox Jews there was a long list of things they could not do, such as driving a car, turning on an electric stove to prepare their food, pushing buttons on an elevator, or turning on electric lights. (Most Orthodox Jews have Sabbath timers on their lights, appliances, and so on. Hotels have Sabbath elevators that stop at every floor—an elevator you don't want to use unless you have to!) The activities they engaged in, the songs they sang, and even some of the foods served at the Shabbat meal were symbolic of spiritual things. Truly their Sabbath was not something just to endure or a day-long inconvenience to get over, but it was a celebration of remembering God and basking in the light of His goodness and grace.

That light was represented by the lighting of the Sabbath candles and the accompanying prayer offered to usher in the Sabbath celebration. We were moved to tears when Rabbi Rosen and his wife, Sharon, tenderly took their children into their arms as part of their weekly Sabbath observance and pronounced a Sabbath blessing, or *Kiddush*, upon them. "God make thee as Ephraim and Manasseh," stated the blessing to the sons; to the daughters, it was, "God make thee as Sarah, Rebekah, Rachel, and Leah." The words that the Rosens spoke to their children also included these blessings from the book of Numbers that are uttered each Sabbath in the synagogue: "The Lord bless thee, and keep thee: The Lord make his face shine upon thee, and be gracious unto thee: The Lord lift up his countenance upon thee, and give thee peace" (Numbers 6:24–26).

Rabbi Rosen further explained to our students that Jews celebrate the Sabbath as a queen coming to visit their homes. It is a joyous event, a covenantal sign, "that ye may know that I am the Lord that doth sanctify you" (Exodus 31:13). A special spice box is also used to represent the sweetness of the Sabbath and the refreshment it is to the soul. At the conclusion of the Sabbath, another candle, the *Havdalah*, is lit. The flame of that candle is extinguished at the end of the Sabbath celebration—representing the conclusion of that which is sacred (Shabbat) and the beginning again of the mundane. These symbols remind devout Jews that Shabbat sanctifies *from* the world and prepares one to live *in* the world. We can have "holy envy" of that.

What a contrast to the way we were too often prone to view the Sabbath! As we watched the Rosens earnestly celebrate Sabbath, we felt chastened for what was sometimes a bad attitude—but most of all we felt regret that we, so often, had cheated ourselves out of the joy they were obviously experiencing. Too frequently, we may fall on the other end of the spectrum. We equate the command "keep the Sabbath day holy" with "thou shalt not"—like the Pharisees of Jesus's day, complete with a long list of "can't dos." Viewing the Sabbath day this way may cause us at times to think of God's commandment to honor His holy day as some form of punishment—kind of like being grounded—instead of seeing it as a day of spiritual rejuvenation and a covenantal reminder of our relationship with God. Even when our Sabbath is filled with much Church service and many meetings, it isn't always a day of "delight," as the prophet Isaiah called it (see Isaiah 58:13). We may not be "breaking the Sabbath" by doing something that we shouldn't—even though Brent often jokes that, at least on Sunday, he is too busy to sin—but maybe, in all our busyness, our approach to the Sabbath lacks intention and the deep spiritual communion with the Lord and our loved ones that our soul craves and the Lord intends for us.

Admittedly, there are many, many proscriptions for the modern-day Orthodox Jews that we don't envy and that don't fit with our understanding of keeping the Sabbath holy. Many of these "forbidden" actions may seem trivial or a distraction to us. But the truth remains that the practitioners of these find joy and holiness in even the smallest of these rituals and restraints. Recently, as we talked with some friends about the Church's renewed emphasis on strengthening our faith in the Lord through more meaningful Sabbath observance, one of our friends confessed that she felt so restricted on Sunday—not knowing exactly what activities would be considered "Sabbath appropriate." Her honest expression of feelings of restriction by traditional Sabbath expectations was not foreign to us. Most all of us at some time or another have had similar feelings. It seems that we have had the "can't dos" reinforced through the years by culture, teachings, and experience. This emphasis on the "restrictions" is almost always well-intentioned and designed to teach the doctrine of the Sabbath. However, we usually are left feeling, like our friend described, restricted, oppressed, guilty, or anxious for the day to end.

As another one of our friends said, "If the Sabbath isn't bringing you joy, then you must be doing it wrong." Our Orthodox Jewish friends have far, far more "can't dos" than we do, yet they find joy—even delight—in Sabbath observance. From them, we have learned that it isn't so much about the *activities*—what you can or can't do—but rather the *attitude*—how we spiritually and emotionally approach God on the Lord's day and what we feel deep within our hearts and souls (see D&C 59:9–13). Whatever we do or don't do, the most important focus we can put on the Sabbath is what happens within ourselves. It should be well thought out, purposeful, and meaningful to us. Whatever it is or is not, it should be consecrated and dedicated to the Lord. Indeed, the essential thing is to "remember the Sabbath day, to keep it *holy*" (Exodus 20:8)—not just different, or restful, or thoughtful, or family-oriented, or a day to attend meetings, though all of those things are vital, but *holy*, between the Lord and us.

What is meant by *holy*? Perhaps we can understand the definition of *holiness* better with examples of things characterized as *holy*. Here are just a few: the *holy* temple, the *holy* scriptures, the *holy* prophets, the *Holy* Ghost, the *Holy* One of Israel. Something or someone *holy* is set apart from the world and worldliness and dedicated solely to the Lord—in the world, but not of it. The Lord literally separated the children of Israel from the rest of the nations in order to make them His. Not only would He be holy to them, they would be holy to Him: "And ye shall be holy unto me: for I the Lord am holy, and have *severed* you from other people, that ye should be mine" (Leviticus 20:26; emphasis added). The word *severed* is an interesting word selected by Bible translators to describe God's people and His day. The Sabbath is severed from the other days of the week to be *holy* to Him. Saints—holy ones—have been severed from the world and dedicated to the Lord, made holy by Him.

In a related passage, the Lord also said, "For I am the Lord your God: ye shall therefore sanctify yourselves, and ye shall be holy; for I am holy" (Leviticus 11:44). If we think of ourselves as "holy ones," how might that shape our Sabbath observance?

Though often termed "the Lord's day," the Sabbath is *our* day, too. It gives us a regular opportunity to devote an entire day to "practic[ing] virtue and holiness" before the Lord (like practicing the piano)—to practice being like Him, practice being with Him, practice bringing others to Him. It also allows us a glimpse of *His* holiness, of heaven, of eternal life with our families. How much harder would it be to be like Him without this sacred blessing? How can we dwell with Him forever if we can't seek holiness for at least one whole day out of a week?

Saints from Adam and Eve to the present day have honored the holiness of the Sabbath. In the next few chapters, we examine the history of the Sabbath and the instructions given to God's children in earlier dispensations—commandments, teachings, gentle reminders, and even stern rebukes at times—all intended to help them increase in faith and to become holy. These have laid the foundation for our own understanding of the Lord's day. We know this foundation will not only *instruct* us in the purposes of the Sabbath and what the Lord intends for us with regard to it, but it can also *inspire* us with a greater view of how it was created to bless us and how we can receive its blessings for ourselves and our families.

CHAPTER 2
The Perpetual Covenant:
A Sign from the Beginning

THE SABBATH IS LITERALLY AS old as the Creation. It is presented as a part of the Creation story sequence, even though no creating took place on that day or during that time period: "Thus the heaven and the earth were finished, and all the host of them. And on the seventh day I, God, ended my work, and all things which I had made; and I rested on the seventh day from all my work. . . ." He further informed us, "And I, God, *blessed* the seventh day, and *sanctified* it; because that in it I had rested from all my work which I, God, had created and made" (Moses 3:1–3; emphasis added).

Since the Lord surely could have rested without telling us about it, this day of rest had some greater meaning for His children. The fact that the Lord included this day as part of the Creation process showcases its significance and meaning as a final, indispensable part of that process—a sign of completion (the number seven represents perfection or completion in the Jewish religion), a mark of approval and acceptance, or a hallowing ordinance-like action and foreordained part of the plan that motivated the Creation itself.

The Sabbath obviously created a pattern of time measurement—but more important, it is a greater symbol of the Lord's eternal course. It may be that on that day, He also taught and prepared Adam and Eve for the work that lay ahead. The Sabbath was a time of sanctification and blessing. In this sense, it makes us wonder if this sacred "day of rest" after the Creation could have been the time when Adam and Eve were endowed from on high, received sacred instructions and covenants, and were sealed for eternity. Of course, we do not know, but it is an interesting thought in light of the original intent of that seventh day.

Regardless of whatever transpired, that first Sabbath would be a reminder and sign pointing Adam and Eve and their posterity to the eternal Sabbath that awaited them if they chose to return to Him. It is this notion of the earthly Sabbath foreshadowing eternal life that is found throughout Jewish rabbinical writings. "According to the Talmud," wrote Rabbi Abraham Joshua Heschel, "the Sabbath is *me'en 'olam ha-ba,* which means *somewhat like* eternity or the world to come."[4]

Moreover, the Lord not only tells us that He rested from His labors that day, but that He "blessed" the day and "sanctified" it, perhaps as the very first holy day, maybe even something like what we would call a holiday to be celebrated. The word *holiday* comes from "holy day" but has lost its "holy" connotation. In addition to Sabbaths, God later ordained frequent and regular holy days or celebrations to be part of Jewish worship. Such holy days helped the Jews worship, commemorate, and recommit to God as well as rest from their labors and gather together, rejoicing as families and as a nation. Holidays, or "holy days," are obviously important to the Lord.

From Adam and Eve to Moses

The scriptures give no explicit record, however, of the Lord ordaining Sabbaths or holy days for Adam and Eve or for any of their posterity after the Fall until Moses and the children of Israel. Yet, the purpose and pattern of the Sabbath would surely imply that they had this sacred, weekly observance. We know they were taught the gospel and the plan of salvation. They worshipped and offered sacrifice in similitude of the sacrifice of Christ (see Abraham 5:6–7). They were clothed with symbolic holy garments (Abraham 4:27) and taught in other figurative ways as well.

Since the keeping of the Sabbath day was so foundational as to be introduced at Creation and to subsequently become the fourth of the Ten Commandments, it only makes sense that this symbolic worship would also have been a part of the original commandments given to Adam and Eve and later passed on by Noah and his family. Surely other faithful communities before the Exodus, such as the cities of Enoch and of Melchizedek, observed a Sabbath. They

---

[4] Heschel, *The Sabbath,* 74.

would have been familiar with the Creation account. It certainly seems that Abraham would have been taught this central principle and would have taught it to his posterity. The children of Abraham, Isaac, and Jacob may have even observed it in Egypt before they were made slaves—at least until the majority fell into apostasy. However, there are hints that a righteous remnant remained who worshipped Jehovah (see Exodus 1:17, 3:13–16, 4:1). Forced to serve as slaves, they were probably rarely allowed to observe Sabbaths. The *Midrash*, a collection of Jewish commentaries, interpretations, and stories concerning the Torah (first five books of the Bible) declares:

> He [Moses] saw that they had no rest, so he went to Pharaoh and said: If one has a slave and he does not give him rest one day in the week he dies; similarly, if thou wilt not give thy slaves one day in the week rest, they will die. Pharaoh replied: Go and do with them as thou sayest. Thereupon Moses ordained for them the Sabbath day for rest.
>   . . . the Israelites possessed scrolls with the contents of which they regaled themselves . . . each Sabbath, assuring them that God would redeem them. Thus because they rested on the Sabbath, Pharaoh said to them: Let heavier work be laid upon the men, that they may labour therein: and let them not regard lying words . . . let them not take delight or rest on the Sabbath day.[5]

As further proof that the Sabbath was not new to them, the children of Israel observed the Sabbath even before they reached Mt. Sinai, where the Ten Commandments were given. In Exodus 16, we read the account of the Lord introducing manna to the people. They are instructed to gather twice as much on the sixth day and not to gather any on the seventh day. "And he said unto them, This *is that* which the Lord hath said, To morrow *is* the rest of the holy sabbath unto the Lord: bake *that* which ye will bake *to day*, and seethe that ye will seethe; and that which remaineth over lay up for you to be kept until the morning" (Exodus 16:23).

---

5 *Midrash Rabbah,* 3rd ed., Rabbi Dr. H. Freedman and Maurice Simon, trans.; London: Soncino Press, 1983, 3:35.

Sabbath does not appear to be a new concept that needs definition here. Many biblical scholars agree: "There is nothing in either text or context that seems to intimate that the Sabbath was now first given to the Israelites, as some have supposed: on the contrary, it is here spoken of as being perfectly well known, from its having been generally observed."[6]

Moses and the Israelites

In any case, the Sabbath was re-enthroned in its rightful place by the finger of the Lord at Mt. Sinai. Engraved by Him on stone tablets, it was introduced to the children of Israel as the fourth of ten basic laws that would become the foundation of Judeo-Christian philosophy. This fourth law focused on their unique relationship to God: "Remember the sabbath day, to keep it holy," it read. "Six days shalt thou labour, and do all thy work: But the seventh day *is* the sabbath of the Lord thy God" (Exodus 20:8–10). At this point, the children of Israel were pointed back to the original Sabbath. "For *in* six days the Lord made heaven and earth, the sea, and all that in them *is*, and rested the seventh day: wherefore the Lord blessed the sabbath day, and hallowed it" (Exodus 20:11). Again, many scholars agree that the Israelites were commanded to "remember" the Sabbath because it had already been known since the beginning of the world.

Celebrating Freedom

The clarification that follows the commandment suggests something else the Israelites must remember: "*in it* thou shalt not do any work, thou, nor thy son, nor thy daughter, thy manservant, nor thy maidservant, nor thy cattle, nor thy stranger that *is* within thy gates" (Exodus 20:10). In other words, they were not to work or cause others to work on the Sabbath; not even the animals should be made to carry burdens on this hallowed day. The Israelites knew what it meant to be forced to work. They had been slaves themselves. Now that they were freed, not only were they to remember their deliverance each Sabbath but to learn mercy by granting that same freedom to all creation. Freeing themselves and others from the

---

6 Adam Clark, *Commentary on the Bible*, 1:386.

demands of the world symbolized this. On the website *Judaism 101*, one commentator explained:

> What does the Exodus have to do with resting on the seventh day? It's all about freedom. As I said before, in ancient times, leisure was confined to certain classes; slaves did not get days off. Thus, by resting on Shabbat, we are reminded that we are free. But in a more general sense, Shabbat frees us from our weekday concerns, from our deadlines and schedules and commitments. During the week, we are slaves to our jobs, to our creditors, to our need to provide for ourselves; on Shabbat, we are freed from these concerns, much as our ancestors were freed from slavery in Egypt.[7]

The Sabbath was repeated regularly so that they could continually remember their freedom from bondage. For us, the Sabbath is a token of our deliverance from the captivity of sin and mortality, and a type of that day to come when these things will trouble us no more. It is a designated time to practice the same liberating mercy that has been extended to us. It is a type of the liberating Atonement of Jesus Christ. With that understanding, who wouldn't celebrate the Sabbath? Perhaps we need a touch of "Independence Day" spirit in our Sabbath observance.

Eternal Consequences

Unlike today, under the law of Moses there was an immediate penalty for working on the Sabbath. The fact that the Lord later decreed that a person was to be put to death for this violation teaches us about its importance and centrality in God's commandments: "Ye shall keep the sabbath therefore; for it is holy unto you: every one that defileth it shall surely be put to death" (Exodus 31:14). Why such a drastic consequence for not honoring the Sabbath day? With this kind of consequence, how can God be loving, and how can his commands be "gentle," as the hymn declares? (See *Hymns*, 125.)

[7] Tracy Rich, *Judaism 101*, www.jewfaq.org/shabbat.htm, accessed December 10, 2015.

Like all aspects of God's law, as given to Moses, the prescribed consequences for disobedience were intended to be symbolic, albeit very literal and physical, of spiritual consequences. The sentence that follows gives us further insight: "for whosoever doeth any work therein, *that soul shall be cut off from among his people*" (Exodus 31:14; emphasis added). An Israelite would be physically cut off from among his people to warn them that they would be spiritually cut off from the Lord's presence if they rejected the covenant of the Sabbath. The message rang loud and clear. Without reverencing the Sabbath, one cannot become holy. Thus, our very eternal lives depend on it.

A Sign between the Lord and His People

Some of the other instruction given to the children of Israel about the Sabbath is also important for us. Moses made a second recorded trip up Mt. Sinai. There the Lord gave Moses instructions for building the tabernacle and preparing Aaron and his sons to do service therein. Just before sending Moses down from Mt. Sinai with the stone tablets (no, he didn't get them the first time), the last thing the Lord reiterated and re-emphasized to Moses was the absolute imperative of keeping the Sabbath holy: "Speak thou also unto the children of Israel, saying, Verily my sabbaths ye shall keep: *for it is a sign between me and you throughout your generations; that ye may know that I am the Lord that doth sanctify you*" (Exodus 31:13; emphasis added).

This was not only a commandment, but a visible sign—an action almost like an ordinance/covenant ceremony—observable to the Israelites, to other people, to God Himself, that they were faithful to Jehovah and not to the multiple gods of the Egyptians or the Chaldeans or Hittites or Ammonites or all of the different –ites that would surround them. It was a mark of His chosen people that set them apart from the world. As the Lord declared to Moses, the Sabbath would be a sign "throughout your generations"—continuing to this very day and His latter-day Church.

As a sign from the Lord to His people, the Sabbath was a holy gift—"the most precious mankind has received from the treasure house of God"[8]—a sacred time dedicated and set apart, just as sacred

---

[8] Heschel, *The Sabbath*, 18.

space is set apart, to be a "temple of time" so to speak, or as Rabbi Heschel characterized it, "holiness in time."[9] The Sabbath, as a gift from God to His children, is a means whereby His heavenly holiness is imparted to mortals here and now. Thus, the Sabbath is a gateway to holiness, not only in time, but also in eternity.

Perhaps we could also compare it to a weekly date between husband and wife in which commitments to one another and to the marriage are renewed. The symbol of Christ as the husband and the Church as His bride is prevalent in the scriptures. The Sabbath was to be a sacred moment just between Him and His beloved ones, to remind them that they had His full attention and devotion in the form of his redemptive sacrifice and love.

They were to commune together, to renew covenants with one another, to remind each other that He was their God and they were His people. He would always and in all ways be with them and bless them. He was a faithful "husband," and He had an eternal Sabbath prepared for His bride, who should prepare herself, be faithful, and reciprocate His love. It was so important to Him that, like a temple sealing, it was to endure "throughout their generations, for a perpetual covenant. It *is* a sign between me and the children of Israel for ever" (Exodus 31:17).

Though the ancient Israelites eventually became unfaithful to their Husband in many ways, this perpetual covenant continues to mark the Jewish people. While other ancient religious groups and ethnicities have faded into history and lost their unique identity, the Jews have endured not only as a people but also as a major world religion. Sabbath is central to the identities of the practicing as well as to many of the non-practicing Jews.

Elder Quentin L. Cook pointed this out in general conference in October 2015, more than five millennia since the founding of the Jewish faith. He told of spending the Friday evening of Shabbat with Jewish friends in New York. He recounted that he and his wife participated in many aspects of Sabbath ritual that we have mentioned here. "As I thought about this event I reflected on the extreme persecution that the Jews have experienced over centuries," remarked Elder Cook. "Clearly, honoring the Sabbath has been 'a

---

9 Heschel, *The Sabbath*, 10.

perpetual covenant,' preserving and blessing the Jewish people in fulfillment of scripture."[10]

In the preface we quoted a well-known Jewish maxim: "The Jews have kept the Sabbath. The Sabbath has kept the Jews." How has observance of the Sabbath preserved the Jews? One scholar has written that the meaning of this maxim goes well beyond mere "Jewish survivalism." She explained, "[It] meant that the regulation of time through the laws of the Sabbath gave the Jews the chance to regroup in communities at the end of every week, and that that regrouping sustained their Jewish identity."[11] Undoubtedly, this same practice likewise contributes immeasurably to the strength of the Latter-day Saints, not only as individuals but also as a church and a Zion people (see D&C 38:27).

The Seven-Year Sabbath Cycle

The Lord also gave other commandments associated with a Sabbath type of worship that are focused on a seven-year cycle and a seven-times-seven- or forty-nine-year cycle. While we do not observe these celebrations today, studying these unusual directives teaches us a lot about what God wants us to understand about the Sabbath and about the kind of God we worship. As we will see, that translates into a type of the Atonement of Jesus Christ.

The Lord is serious about rest. Rest is ordained of God. This in itself tells us about His generous concern and compassion for us. Even though He told Adam that he would get his nourishment only by the sweat of his brow throughout his entire life (see Genesis 3:19), He lovingly commanded that there be one day out of every seven for relief from that constant, grinding toil. To emphasize the meaning of Sabbath rest, the Lord gave the children of Israel two extra layers of Sabbath observance in which the land itself would also rest: "And six years thou shalt sow thy land, and shalt gather in the fruits thereof,"

[10] "Shipshape and Bristol Fashion: Be Temple Worthy—in Good Times and Bad Times," *Ensign*, November 2015, 41.

[11] Judith Shulevitz, "Remember the Sabbath," Forward.com, *Opinion*; forward.com/opinion/126978/remember-the-sabbath/, March 31, 2010, accessed December 10, 2015.

the Lord directed Moses, "But the seventh *year* thou shalt let it rest and lie still; that the poor of thy people may eat: and what they leave the beasts of the field shall eat. In like manner thou shalt deal with thy vineyard, *and* with thy oliveyard" (Exodus 23:10–11). A day of rest may have seemed like a nice break from work to some, but this was a whole different layer of meaning. Now the Lord was going to test their faith for a whole year at a time. Instead of relying on their own efforts in the seventh year, they were to rely completely on whatever the land alone, blessed by the Lord, would produce.

Later, again on Mt. Sinai, the Lord elaborated on this law that was to be practiced after the Israelites were granted the lands of their inheritance in the promised land. Not only were they not to plant in the seventh year, they were not to cultivate, prune, weed, harvest, store, trade, or sell what the land produced: "That which groweth of its own accord of thy harvest thou shalt not reap, neither gather the grapes of thy vine undressed: *for* it is a year of rest unto the land" (Leviticus 25:5). Landowners were to live spontaneously off the land just as the poor did. "And the sabbath of the land [whatever the land produces by itself] shall be meat for you; for thee, and for thy servant, and for thy maid, and for thy hired servant, and for thy stranger that sojourneth with thee" (Leviticus 25:6). Everyone would be equal in this way, including the livestock: "And for thy cattle, and for the beast that are in thy land, shall all the increase thereof be meat" (Leviticus 25:7).

Actually, God would test the Israelites for more than just one year out of seven. By the time they harvested their first crop after the Sabbath year, it would actually be for a period of about three years or growing seasons: "Then I will command my blessing upon you in the sixth year, and it shall bring forth fruit for three years. And ye shall sow the eighth year, and eat *yet* of old fruit until the ninth year; until her fruits come in ye shall eat *of* the old store" (Leviticus 25:21–22). What was the Lord trying to teach about the concept of Sabbath?

The Jubilee

There are many symbols and meanings found in the Sabbatical cycle described in the Old Testament. In addition to the "Sabbath of Sabbaths," the Jubilee Year is the third layer of Sabbath observance ordained by the Lord. The Lord instructed Moses: "And thou shalt number seven sabbaths of years unto thee, seven times seven years; and the space of the seven sabbaths of years shall be unto thee forty and nine years. . . . And ye shall hallow the fiftieth year" (Leviticus 25:8, 10). In addition to allowing the land to lie fallow while depending on the mercies of the Lord, in the fiftieth year they were commanded to "proclaim liberty throughout *all* the land unto all the inhabitants thereof: it shall be a jubilee unto you; and ye shall return every man unto his possession, and ye shall return every man unto his family" (Leviticus 25:10).

In addition to being forgiven of their debts, the poor were restored to their lands of inheritance that may have been lost through carelessness or misfortune. Israelites who had sold themselves into servitude to pay their debts were set free because, the Lord declared, "they *are* my servants, which I brought forth out of the land of Egypt: they shall not be sold as bondmen" (Leviticus 25:42). Every fifty years was to be a fresh start, a brand new redemption, that would keep the land equally distributed and thereby encourage greater equality among God's people. The rich would not become too rich, nor the poor too poor. God's people were not to get too attached to their lands and possessions because they were only borrowing them: "For the land *is* mine; for ye *are* strangers and sojourners with me" (Leviticus 25:23), the Lord reminded them. Meanwhile, the land itself could rest, regenerate, and become even more productive under the blessing of God that would be bestowed upon it.

Can you see what the Lord was trying to teach His children by implementing these Sabbaths and the provisions that attended them? What was He revealing to them about Himself, His love, His Atonement, His kingdom on earth and in heaven? Here are some of the eye-opening principles we have learned from these Old Testament Sabbath laws and practices that may seem archaic to many:

—Spiritual rest and refreshment is divine. It regenerates us and makes us more productive, not less.

—The Sabbath is an opportunity to renew faith and trust in God, to practice total reliance on the Lord by ceasing from our own efforts to control the world around us.

—The Lord is especially mindful of those who are physically and spiritually poor and needy. They are always on His mind. They are a holy trust and a test for those who have more. We should be especially mindful of what we can do to relieve burdens on the Sabbath, including physical burdens.

—The earth is the Lord's and the fulness thereof; He will provide in abundance if we observe the Sabbath. (This is an economic law, just as is paying tithing and caring for the poor.)

—All are equal in the Lord's sight, including strangers and, as the word is sometimes translated, *Gentiles*. His Atonement is for everyone. His love is the same for everyone. Ours must be also.

—Love, compassion, caring for one another, and unity are essential for God's kingdom—just as all are equal in the temple.

—Christ has redeemed and continues to redeem us from the slavery of sin and death. His Atonement is perfect just as His love and compassion are perfect. Every Sabbath can be a fresh start. We can come back to our roots as sons and daughters of Christ (Mosiah 5:7–8), His redeemed. We can repent and forgive as we are always forgiven.

—We are here on earth through the mercy of Christ. Of ourselves we own nothing. Without Him, we are nothing, yet through Him and because of His perfect love for us, He gives us all He has and we become what He is. This is love and mercy that seems impossible to fathom. Perhaps this is why He gives us work that is a type of His work.

—We should come together with our families and in our congregations to rejoice in the Lord and celebrate His Sabbath by worshipping and strengthening spiritual ties to Him and to each other. We should strive for spiritual equality.

As with us today, as the Israelites honored these commandments and understood their greater meaning, the blessings and the special favor of the Lord were upon them. Their covenant with Jehovah was in force, and they grew in the beauty of holiness (see Psalm 96:9). Yet it seems that, more often than not, they did not practice what they promised (hopefully not like us today). Prophets were continually calling them back to their Savior, reminding them of the redemption that was to have ransomed them from the slavery of sin and made them holy. The Sabbath was a sign that they were called to a higher life than other people. Their neglect in keeping the Sabbath was a sign that they had rejected their Redeemer. Isaiah excoriated his people for their disingenuous observance of the fast and the Sabbath, which have similar purposes and could be interchangeable in this passage:

> Shout it aloud, do not hold back.
> Raise your voice like a trumpet.
> Declare to my people their rebellion
> and to the descendants of Jacob their sins.
> For day after day they seek me out;
> they seem eager to know my ways,
> as if they were a nation that does what is right
> and has not forsaken the commands of its God.
> They ask me for just decisions
> and seem eager for God to come near them.
> "Why have we fasted," they say,
> "and you have not seen it?
> Why have we humbled ourselves,
> and you have not noticed?"
>
> Yet on the day of your fasting [Sabbath], you do as you please
> and exploit all your workers.
> Your fasting ends in quarreling and strife,
> and in striking each other with wicked fists.
> You cannot fast as you do today
> and expect your voice to be heard on high.
> Is this the kind of fast I have chosen,
> only a day for people to humble themselves?
> Is it only for bowing one's head like a reed
> and for lying in sackcloth and ashes?
> Is that what you call a fast,
> a day acceptable to the Lord?
>
> Is not this the kind of fasting I have chosen:
> to loose the chains of injustice

and untie the cords of the yoke,
to set the oppressed free
and break every yoke?
Is it not to share your food with the hungry
and to provide the poor wanderer with shelter—
when you see the naked, to clothe them,
and not to turn away from your own flesh and blood?
(Isaiah 58:1–7, *New International Version*)

Other prophets complained of similar negligence. The Lord labored long with them—hundreds of years—giving them every possible chance to repent. Finally, their special relationship with Jehovah was squandered. The Northern Kingdom of Israel fell in 722 BC, and about 150 years later, the Southern Kingdom of Judah also fell. Even as destruction was at their doors, the Lord, through the prophet Jeremiah, gave them one last opportunity: "If ye diligently hearken unto me . . . to bring in no burden through the gates of this city on the sabbath day, but *hallow the sabbath day, to do no work therein* . . . this city shall remain for ever" (Jeremiah 17:24–25; emphasis added). Unfortunately, he reports, "they obeyed not, neither inclined their ear, but made their neck stiff, that they might not hear, nor receive instruction" (Jeremiah 17:23).

From exile in Babylon, Ezekiel lamented the infidelity that had landed the Israelites in captivity once again: "Her priests have violated my law [as one commentator observed, "violated—not simply transgressed; but, have done violence to the law, by wresting it to wrong ends, and putting wrong constructions on it],[12] and have profaned mine holy things." He then explains what He means: "They have put no difference between the holy and profane [common], neither have they shewed difference between the unclean and the clean, and *have hid their eyes from my sabbaths*, and I am profaned among them" (Ezekiel 22:23; emphasis added). In other words, they treated the Sabbath just like every other day and had become just like every other people. It is also interesting that in the verses before and after this passage the Lord again forcefully condemns Israel for

---

[12] *Jamieson-Fausset-Brown Bible Commentary* on biblehub.com/ezekiel/22-26.htm, accessed January 5, 2016.

its greedy exploitation of the poor—again the treatment of the poor and the neglect of the Sabbath are linked together. "Therefore have I poured out mine indignation upon them," the Lord concludes ominously. "Their own way have I recompensed upon their heads" (Ezekiel 22:31).

Later, after seventy years in captivity, some Jews were allowed to return to Jerusalem to rebuild the temple and the walls of the city. The prophet Nehemiah was one of them. He, like prophets before him, struggled to help his people understand that they were not like other nations. When he saw them treading their wine presses, working their lands, and trading with foreign merchants on the Sabbath, he diligently labored to reinstate the holiness of the Sabbath in their consciousness. "Did not your fathers thus, and did not our God bring all this evil upon us, and upon this city?" he chided them. "Yet ye bring more wrath upon Israel by profaning the Sabbath" (Nehemiah 13:18).

Concerned that they would once again suffer the consequences of betraying the Lord, he ordered the gates of the newly rebuilt walls of Jerusalem closed on the Sabbath and drove away the merchants who set up shop outside the walls (see Nehemiah 13:19–22). Sabbath-keeping was obviously a key measurement of the faithfulness of God's people. Obedience to the fourth commandment was both protection and strength.

Nehemiah and others of the prophets of that generation must have been successful to some extent, because by the time of Christ almost five hundred years later, Sabbath observance, at least outwardly, was a well-established and central facet of first-century Jewish life. Unlike Nehemiah, Ezekiel, Jeremiah, Isaiah, and others of the prophets, Jesus did not have to call the people to repentance for totally neglecting Sabbath observance. However, he had to call them to repentance because, by their traditions and overzealousness, they had lost much of the spiritual meaning of the Sabbath and original intent of the holy day. In the next chapter, we will examine how Jesus, the Master Teacher and Lord of the Sabbath, sought to restore that sacred knowledge.

CHAPTER 3
"Lord of the Sabbath"
Jesus Restores the True Meaning

BY THE TIME CHRIST'S MORTAL ministry began, the Sabbath had become an elaborately defined and often burdensome institution among the Jews. Well-meaning Pharisees and perhaps others had developed "fences," or preventative observances, around every aspect of the law of Moses. While such "fences around the law" may have initially been established to protect people from disobedience, these new expectations soon became overly legalistic.

The "traditions of the elders," as Jesus called these "fences," sought to anticipate any possible way whereby a person could violate the law. As a result, they soon included a long list of activities that were forbidden in any form in an attempt to ensure that no one would get anywhere near the edge. As we read in the Gospel accounts recorded in the New Testament, these traditions of the Jewish leaders (most often identified in the scriptures as scribes and Pharisees) came into conflict with the teachings and actions of Christ with regard to honoring the Sabbath.

Not only did these traditions cause the Jewish leaders to misunderstand the meaning and purpose of the Sabbath, but it caused them to misjudge and condemn those who didn't meet their stringent standards. This included their own Messiah, who—as "Lord of the Sabbath" (Matthew 12:8) and Jehovah of the Old Testament—gave the Sabbath and the law of Moses to their ancestors (see 3 Nephi 15:5–10). They were, as the Book of Mormon prophet Jacob said, "looking beyond the mark" (Jacob 4:14).

"Looking Beyond the Mark":
Missing the True Meaning of the Sabbath

This looking beyond the mark—missing the target, purpose, and true meaning of something—is most evident in the traditional "fences around the law" that had crept into belief and practice among many of the Jews in Jesus's day. The Savior often confronted this spiritual shortsightedness and condemned superficial, legalistic, and laborious observances that "missed the point."

While not speaking specifically of the Sabbath but of other similar legalistic observances, the Savior condemned such behavior when the Pharisees confronted Him by asking, "Why walk not thy disciples according to the tradition of the elders?" With His answer, Christ re-indicted them for the same hypocrisy their ancestors were guilty of centuries earlier: "Well hath Esaias [Isaiah] prophesied of you hypocrites, as it is written, This people honoureth me with their lips, but their heart is far from me. . . . In vain do they worship me, teaching for doctrines the commandments of men." He concluded with this broad condemnation: "Full well ye reject the commandment of God, that ye may keep your own tradition" (Mark 7:5–7, 9).

The Master went on to teach those who would listen that holiness—which is the desired outcome of the law and every commandment of God—comes from within, not from without. Outward performances alone are empty, and when they are done to impress or deceive others and satisfy our pride, they are sinful. In his classic work, *The Life of Christ*, Frederic W. Farrar insightfully captured what Jesus was teaching about the Sabbath and other commandments that had become distorted and overly legalistic and behavioral, rather than deeply spiritual through the "traditions of the elders":

> It is easy to be a slave to the letter, and difficult to enter into the spirit; easy to obey a number of outward rules, difficult to enter intelligently and self-sacrificingly into the will of God; easy to entangle the soul in a network of petty observances, difficult to yield the obedience of an enlightened heart; easy to be haughtily exclusive, difficult to be humbly spiritual; easy to be an ascetic or

a formalist, difficult to be pure and loving, and wise, and free; easy to be a Pharisee, difficult to be a disciple; very easy to embrace a self-satisfying and sanctimonious system of rabbinical observances, very difficult to love God with all the heart, and all the might, and all the soul, and all the strength.[13]

Interestingly, many of the miracles performed by the Savior during his mortal ministry, as recorded in the Gospels, occurred on the Sabbath. No doubt, the Savior did this intentionally as a backdrop to His testimony of Himself as the "Lord of the Sabbath" and His condemnation of the mark-missing hypocrisy of scribes and Pharisees who had transformed the simple, sanctifying power of the Sabbath into a complex mess of rules that were more burdens than blessings. As He exposed this and called the guilty to repentance, He was able to teach the true meaning and help restore to the people a vision of the Sabbath through His Father's eyes.

From the Savior's miracles, reproofs, and teachings we learn that hypocritical Sabbath-keeping is, in reality, Sabbath-breaking. It violates the spirit and purpose of the Sabbath: an opportunity to draw nearer to God through worship and service.

The very Giver of the Sabbath taught on another occasion, "The sabbath was made for man, and not man for the sabbath" (Mark 2:27). It was intended to relieve their mortal burdens, to free them to focus on spirituality and service, and to help them become ready to receive the greater eternal gifts that await them. The requirements of the Pharisees did the opposite by laying "grievous" burdens that, as the Savior said, they themselves were not willing to touch with one of their fingers" (see Luke 11:46).

So rigid were their traditions that they would even seek to prevent the very Son of God from healing on His own day and seek to put Him to death when He did so. One synagogue leader was indignant when on the Sabbath Christ healed a woman who had been "bowed together" (bent over) for eighteen years. Luke says she "could in no wise lift up herself"—an apt metaphor for all the rest of us in

---

[13] Frederic W. Farrar, *The Life of Christ* (1875; reprint, Salt Lake City: Bookcraft, 1994), 445.

our spiritual infirmities. "There are six days in which men ought to work," scolded the synagogue ruler. "In them therefore come and be healed, and not on the Sabbath day" (Luke 13:10–17). Apparently, miraculous healing was one of those activities forbidden on the Sabbath by the Pharisees. Perhaps the synagogue leader expected Jesus to tell the woman, "Could you please come back tomorrow for your miracle?"

To put this in context and to highlight the questions with which Jesus wants the people to struggle as He performs healings on the Sabbath, it is important to know that any form of "work" on the Sabbath was forbidden. As you can imagine, it is difficult to define with precision what constitutes *work*. The scribes and Pharisees (and later rabbis) sought to not only define *work*, but to put all possible *work* activities into categories, resulting in thirty-nine categories. Then it became necessary to anticipate every kind of activity that could humanly be done on the Sabbath and determine if it fit into one of those categories. For example, one of the categories is "finishing," which means that any form of adjustment or repair to another article would be forbidden. Under this provision, sharpening a knife, putting the finishing touches on an article of clothing, or even putting new laces in a shoe would be a violation of the law prohibiting work on the Sabbath. Interestingly, modern religious Jews will not tear toilet paper on the Sabbath but use only pre-cut paper.[14]

You can see how even well-intentioned interpretations and zealous traditions can go amok. While we don't know all of the "rules" that were imposed on the Jews of Jesus's day, we *can* confidently say that they were myriad. Instead of relying on the numerous traditions and oft-conflicting interpretations, Jesus desired His disciples to really ask only two questions: 1) Is it work? and 2) Is it doing good? If it is really work, then you shouldn't do it. If it is doing good, then you should. Work is unlawful by the law, but doing good on the Sabbath is not only lawful, but expected.

On one occasion, Christ encountered a man at the pool of Bethesda who had suffered for thirty-eight years. He had no friends

14 Aryeh Kaplan, *Sabbath—Day of Eternity* (New York: National Conference of Synagogue Youth/Union of Orthodox Jewish Congregations of America, 1974), 32–45.

or family to help him into the pool when the waters bubbled up with their supposedly miraculous healing powers. Such a scenario would melt the hardest of hearts, but not so the hearts of the Pharisees. Christ healed the man and commanded him to pick up his bed and walk for the first time in thirty-eight years. He could finally have a life!

This healing dramatically demonstrated that Jesus of Nazareth—in contrast to the mythological Greek god of healing, Asclepius, who had been worshipped at this very pool in earlier centuries—was God incarnate and had real, verifiable, life-changing, healing power. But what was the Pharisees' "take" on this miracle? They immediately chastised the man for carrying his bed, because carrying "burdens" on the Sabbath was forbidden by the law of Moses. When the man explained that he was told to do it by the One who healed him, they set out to find and put to death the evil criminal who had done such an unforgivable thing by violating the Sabbath.

Should all kinds of work cease on the Sabbath? Is healing a violation of God's holy day? No, of course not. Holiness includes good *works*. Hands that serve are more holy than lips that pray.

Anxious to pounce on any perceived imperfection in Jesus, many of the scribes and Pharisees condemned His every act of healing or service performed on the Sabbath. In each instance they were completely blind—"looking beyond the mark"—to the astounding demonstration of pure love and divine power they had witnessed. Moreover, they seemed totally devoid of any feeling of charity for the liberated victim or for the victim's jubilant loved ones.

Obviously, the scribes and Pharisees were oblivious to the meaning of the Sabbath. On more than one occasion, they had the jaw-dropping audacity to confront Christ about whether it was "lawful" to perform a healing miracle on the Sabbath day. With patience and restraint He pointed out to them that if their sheep needed rescue on the Sabbath, they certainly would do it, and rightfully so. How much more true, then, would that be of a human being who needed rescuing or healing from pain or sin (see Matthew 12:10)? He could have condemned them; instead, He taught them.

The principal thing to note is that Christ was indeed willing to compromise a lesser or outward observance in order to meet the higher purpose of the Sabbath. Notice this is just the opposite of the Pharisees, who were willing to compromise God's laws to keep their own traditions. On another occasion, Christ pointed out to them that they were willing to circumcise (a good work) on the Sabbath so as not to violate the law of Moses requiring circumcision on the eighth day. Yet they would prevent Him from making someone whole (an even greater work) on the Sabbath (see John 7:23).

When the Pharisees challenged Him because His disciples "threshed" wheat (by rubbing it between their hands) to get some sustenance on the Sabbath day, Christ's reply affirms that they had lost their common sense along with the higher purposes of the law of Moses. Their own scriptures testified against them. Did they not remember how their beloved King David and his men had been allowed to eat the holy bread of the temple (normally only for priests) when they took refuge in the temple and were hungry? (See Matthew 12:3–4.) Under their own law, priests labored, offering sacrifice in the temple on the Sabbath and were held blameless (see Matthew 12:5). "But I say unto you," Christ warned, "That in this place is *one* greater than the temple" (Matthew 12:6). While Christ may not have expected them to understand that statement, there was something they should have understood because it came from the scriptures they professed to know. He continued, "But if ye had known what *this* meaneth, I will have mercy, and not sacrifice, ye would not have condemned the guiltless" (Matthew 12:7; see also Hosea 6:6). In other words, their daily sacrifices and rituals availed them nothing because they did not produce the love and mercy they were intended to evoke.

Sabbath is not about being stringent in our compliance only to condemn others because they don't meet our supposed standard. We comply according to our conscience, circumstances, and ability. We look for ways to help, bless, uplift, and relieve burdens and forgive others, not condemn them. Likewise, the Savior's Atonement is not about expecting us to perform perfectly but to eventually possess the love and mercy He possesses.

The writers of the Gospels often found it important to point out that healings took place on the Sabbath, even though they undoubtedly took place every day of the week. In addition to those already mentioned, on the Sabbath day the Lord also cast out demons (see Luke 4:33–36), healed a blind man (see John 9:1–14), restored a withered hand (see Matthew 12:9–15), and cured dropsy (see Luke 14:1–6)—and these are only the *recorded* miracles. There can be no doubt that there were countless more of every sort, both temporal and spiritual. Clearly, Christ had something higher and better to teach the Jews and all of us about the Sabbath.

Our family found ourselves in one of these dilemmas addressed by the Savior many years ago when our children were younger. We often traveled to Idaho from our home in Utah to visit grandparents for the weekend and stay with them. Often we went for reunions or other family or friend activities or commitments. Our time on Friday night and Saturday was often gobbled up, and before we knew it, Sunday was upon us. We attended church and then began the four-hour drive home.

One spring weekend passed in just that way. On Sunday morning we were about to get dressed for church when Wendy's widowed mother, who was not active in the Church, asked if we would help her till a soil supplement into her substantially sized garden before we returned to Utah. The work was simply too strenuous for her to do. Unfortunately, we didn't have time to attend church, do the job for her, and get home on time. There was no way on earth we were going to say, "Sorry, we have to attend our church meetings," or, "Sorry, we don't work on the Sabbath." Nor did we believe that the Savior would have been pleased with such a pharisaical response.

We put on our work clothes and went to work. It was one of the best Sabbath days ever because we sacrificed our pride. Had others seen us they may well have questioned our commitment to the gospel, but we knew that "Pure religion and undefiled before God and the Father is this, To visit the fatherless and widows in their affliction." Such occasions have been rare, and we need the spiritual maturity to recognize them and to discern our own motives, because the second part of the definition of pure, undefiled religion is this, "to keep [ourselves] unspotted from the world" (James 1:27)—one of the main purposes of the Sabbath and especially the sacrament (see D&C 59:9).

That being said, Christ seems to have "worked" very hard on Sabbath days. What was He teaching us through His divine example about the best way to observe the Sabbath? He worshipped and attended synagogue. He read scriptures (see Mark 6:2). He bore testimony and taught the gospel to groups and individuals. He strengthened faith and lifted burdens of pain and suffering. He set others free from sin and torment. We can surmise that He practiced other things He preached as well. Undoubtedly, He rested on occasion but was never indolent. He spent time with family and loved ones but never without leaving them lifted. Certainly He spent time with children and women, the second-class citizens of that day, and with the dejected and rejected. He may have traveled farther than the traditional "Sabbath day's journey" (Acts 1:12) prescribed by the Pharisees, but surely it was only to be of further service and blessing to others. In other words, He "worked," but He did His Father's works and not His own (see John 5:17).

In contrast to the complex, burdensome system of Sabbath prohibitions imposed by the "traditions of the elders," Jesus restored a true understanding of the divinely simple, yet deeply sanctifying purposes of the Sabbath as God intended it from the beginning. "Wherefore the Sabbath was given to man," declared the Master, "for a day of rest; and also that man should glorify God" (JST, Mark 2:26). No need for thirty-nine categories and countless legal interpretations—just two principles and the Spirit of God. We are to "rest" and "glorify God."

These two principles are the ideals toward which we can work toward and after which we pattern our Sabbaths—pure religion undefiled before God. Our Sabbath work is to do God's work— to physically and mentally rest from our labors and "glorify God by doing His will." It is to invite God's presence into our hearts and homes. It is to imitate Christ at least this one day—to put aside self-centered motives and personal desires, whatever the activity or inactivity, and give ourselves to the Lord. And as with all commandments, righteous motivation is at the heart of righteous observance. Hopefully, we choose to do the right things for the right reasons, the most important reason being how much we love and adore the Lord. That is the holiness we seek on His holy day.

CHAPTER 4
"Belonging to the Lord"
Sunday Becomes the Lord's Day

ALTHOUGH THERE ARE FEW ACCOUNTS in the New Testament of Jesus delivering specific doctrinal teachings regarding the Sabbath, accounts of His actions regarding that holy day are clearly recorded with deliberate purpose. The Gospels, written decades after His death and Resurrection, may have been seeking to emphasize the differences between Christians and Jews, confirming that unlike Jews, who revered the law, Christians followed the risen Lord.

As the gospel spread increasingly to Gentiles, Judaizers lost power in the early Church. Christians began to understand that the law of Moses had truly been fulfilled in Christ and that even former Jews were no longer under its requirements. With this realization, some began to question the observance of the Sabbath, a practice unique to Judaism. And as they were increasingly identified with yet persecuted by Jews, Christians sought to distance themselves from the observance of the Sabbath on the seventh day.

For many years after the resurrection of Christ, most converts were Jews and continued to attend synagogue and observe the Sabbath. They continued to be identified with the Jews. As seen in the book of Acts, there are several mentions of Paul preaching in synagogues on the Sabbath, even decades later. Yet these first-century disciples of Christ, in addition to worshipping in the synagogue, met separately on other days in private homes to partake of the eucharist (the Lord's Supper), to partake of a communal feast of fellowship, and to preach the gospel and strengthen each other (see 1 Corinthians 11; Acts 2:47; 20:7). This practice eventually gravitated to Sunday in remembrance of the day Christ rose from the tomb. As early Christians began to separate themselves from Judaism and formalized more distinct Christian worship on Sunday, they viewed that day as the "true Sabbath." By about AD 90, when John, the beloved Apostle of Christ, penned his revelation, he referred to Sunday as "the Lord's day," as it had come to be known.

One of the earliest Christian fathers wrote the following description of Christian worship on Sunday:

> And **on the day called Sunday**, all who live in cities or in the country gather together to one place, and the memoirs of the apostles or the writings of the proph- ets are read, as long as time permits; then, when the reader has ceased, the president verbally instructs, and exhorts to the imitation of these good things. Then we all rise together and pray, and, as we before said, when our prayer is ended, bread and wine and water are brought, and the president in like manner offers prayers and thanksgivings, according to his ability, and the people assent, saying Amen; and there is a distribu- tion to each, and a participation of that over which thanks have been given, and to those who are absent a portion is sent by the deacons. And they who are well to do, and willing, give what each thinks fit; and what is collected is deposited with the president, who suc- cors the orphans and widows and those who, through sickness or any other cause, are in want, and those who are in bonds and the strangers sojourning among us, and in a word takes care of all who are in need. But **Sunday is the day on which we all hold our common assembly, because it is the first day on which God, having wrought a change in the darkness and mat- ter, made the world; and Jesus Christ our Savior on the same day rose from the dead.** For He was cruci- fied on the day before that of Saturn (Saturday); and on the day after that of Saturn, which is the day of the Sun, having appeared to His apostles and disciples, He

taught them these things, which we have submitted to
you also for your consideration.[15]

As evidenced by Justin and other authors in the early Christian
church, by the fourth century the church regularly observed Sunday
as its true Sabbath. Christian scholars sought to justify and give
meaning to this shift. Some suggested it was to parallel the first
day of creation, when light was separated from darkness—Christ's
Resurrection being the beginning of "new creation" and "new light."
Another interpretation posits that the Jewish Sabbath marked the
end of the Lord's creative work, and that Christ's Resurrection on the
first day marked the beginning of His redemptive work. Some early
Christian fathers suggested that under the higher law, the purpose of
the Sabbath day had been fulfilled in Christ; they even argued that
every day should be a Sabbath. Whatever their thinking, Christians
had distanced themselves from Saturday as the Sabbath.

Through the centuries, the importance of Sabbath-keeping waxed
and waned as proponents for and against did battle. Many religious
thinkers and reformers viewed Sabbath observance as a part of the
Mosaic law that had been fulfilled in Christ and, as such, was no
longer necessary. Instead, they argued for a Sabbath that was part of
what they called "natural law." Let's examine a few of these arguments
and the insights contained in them that may help us to better
understand and observe the Lord's day.

Thomas Aquinas taught that the Decalogue (Ten Commandments)
is an expression of natural or moral law that binds all men at all times.
Therefore, along with the other nine commandments, the Sabbath
commandment is a moral requirement. Thus, Sunday rest and worship
became more closely associated with a Christian application of Sabbath
principles, a development toward the idea of a unique "Christian
Sabbath" rather than a Jewish one. Over time, Christians rejected
the legalism of the Jewish Sabbath yet applied the commandment to
"keep the Sabbath" as a reminder that the Christian life—the call to
holiness—is not restricted to a single day, but should be a continuous
pursuit.

---

[15] Justin Martyr, *First Apology*, 67:354–355; emphasis added.

"The new law," Justin Martyr wrote, "requires you to keep the perpetual Sabbath, and you, because you are idle for one day, suppose you are pious, not discerning why this [keeping the Lord's day holy] has been commanded you."[16] Martyr further elaborated that outward observances of the Mosaic Sabbath and other laws do not bring holiness. Only faith in the Lord Jesus Christ, repentance, and "clean hands and a pure heart" yield that.

In the centuries that followed, there was much debate on the extent to which Sabbath (Lord's day) worship was a requirement or expectation for a Christian. Some even suggested that in light of the notion of a "perpetual Sabbath," no amount of Sunday worship or sacrament was required. It may be nice, but it was not necessary. The great reformer and founder of Methodism, John Wesley, spoke of how Christ's Atonement fulfilled—or as he characterized it, "blotted out, took away, and nailed to the cross"—the Mosaic law. "But the moral law contained in the Ten Commandments, and enforced by the prophets, He did not take away. . . . The moral law stands on entirely different foundation from the ceremonial or ritual law. . . . Every part of this law must remain in force upon all mankind in all ages."[17]

There were others, however, who viewed Christ's atoning grace as the ultimate liberty from observances and ordinances, including what we would see as Sabbath worship and rest. As many Christians through the centuries turned away from traditional Sunday worship and "Sabbath-day behaviors," there arose movements that sought to have Christians return to a more holy Sunday worship—both in actions and attitudes. Calvinists and Puritans were among those who sought for a more holy Sunday. In the *Westminster Confession of Faith* we read:

> As it is the law of nature, that, in general, a due pro-
> portion of time be set apart for the worship of God;
> so, in his Word, but a positive, moral and perpetual
> commandment binding all men in all ages, [God] hath

[16] Justin Martyr, *Dialogue with Trypho*, 12.

[17] John Wesley, *On the Sermon on the Mount*, Discourse 6, Sermons on Several Occasions (1810), 75–76.

particularly appointed one day in seven, for a Sabbath, to be kept holy unto him. . . .

This Sabbath is then kept holy unto the Lord, when men, after a due preparing of their hearts, and ordering of their common affairs beforehand, do not only observe a holy rest, all the day, from their own works, words, and thoughts about their worldly employments and recreations, but also are taken up, the whole time, in the public and private exercises of his worship, and in the duties of necessity and mercy.[18]

Contemporary Christianity reflects these centuries-old debates. There is wide diversity of belief and practice in Christian denominations and churches today. The teachings of early Christian fathers, reformers, religious leaders, and great thinkers through the ages have not crystallized the doctrine of the Sabbath. Although we can gain insight from the faithful women and men of past ages who sought to better understand what role the Lord's day should play in the hearts, minds, and daily lives of believers, we must look to prophets and apostles for clarity. Just as the centuries of misinterpretation and misapplication of the doctrine of the fourth commandment led Jesus to "restore" the true meaning of the Sabbath in His day, we look to the Restoration in our day for the "plain and precious truths" regarding Sabbath worship that will yield saving faith and the abundant life.

From the New Testament (and comments of early Christian fathers), there is a valuable insight regarding the Sabbath. It is a concept that bridges the dispensations—helps us to more fully understand the meaning of the Sabbath in times past, but also serves to point us to the ultimate aim of the Lord's day. It is the Greek word in the New Testament—in John's book of Revelation, to be exact—that translates in English as "the Lord's day" (see Revelation 1:10). *Kurios* in Greek means "Lord" or "Master." *Kuriake* means *"belonging to the Lord."* The Holy Sabbath is the Lord's day. It belongs to Him. What we do, what we feel, how we worship, and how we serve on the Lord's day all belong to Him. When the Sabbath day, as the Lord

18 "Of Religious Worship and the Sabbath Day," Chapter 21 in *Westminster Confession of Faith* (1646), 7–8.

intended it, becomes a part of our very soul—the center of our hearts and homes—we, too, become *kuriake*, or "belonging to the Lord."

Let us now consider what this all means to us today. How can we honor and reverence the Lord's day in a way that acknowledges His "ownership" of the day? How can our Sabbath observance and worship more fully bring about our "belonging to the Lord?"

CHAPTER 5
The Sabbath:
Guardian of Faith

PRESIDENT BRIGHAM YOUNG TAUGHT THAT Latter-day Saints observe the Sabbath "for our own temporal good and spiritual welfare." How is that so? Honoring the Lord's day acts as a guardian of faith, a protective power, and the means whereby we keep in remembrance "our God and our holy religion." Why do we assemble each week in church to worship, pray, sing, teach, serve, and learn? Why is there so much emphasis on individuals and families to make the Sabbath a day of delight, holy to the Lord—a day wholly "set apart" from the others, an entire day consecrated to God? Because, as Brother Brigham declared, "we are liable to forget—so prone to wander that we need to have the Gospel sounded in our ears, once, twice, thrice a week, or, behold, we will turn again to our idols."[19] Those who dishonor the Sabbath, Brigham warned, "are weak in the faith," because "gradually, little by little, little by little, the spirit of their religion leaks out of their hearts and their affections."[20]

Certainly Brigham Young's teachings about the Sabbath reflect those of the Prophet Joseph Smith and the revelations of the Restoration. The Saints were taught that the Sabbath was a "holy day" given to man as a divine gift that protectively "plugs" the hole in the hearts of natural men so that, as Brigham Young stated, faith and the "spirit of [our] religion" does not leak out.

"Thou shalt love the Lord thy God with all thy heart, with all thy might, mind, and strength," the Savior declared in a revelation to the

---

[19] Brigham Young, *Journal of Discourses*, 6:195.

[20] Ibid., 15:83.

Prophet Joseph Smith, reiterating the law and commandments given to Moses on the Mount and reaffirmed by Jesus in the meridian of time. "And in the name of Jesus Christ thou shalt serve him."

> Thou shalt love thy neighbor as thyself. Thou shalt not steal; neither commit adultery, nor kill, nor do anything like unto it.
> Thou shalt thank the Lord thy God in all things.
> Thou shalt offer a sacrifice unto the Lord thy God in righteousness, even that of a broken heart and contrite spirit.
> And that thou mayest more fully keep thyself unspotted from the world, thou shalt go to the house of prayer and offer up thy sacraments upon my holy day;
> For verily this is a day appointed unto you to rest from your labors, and to pay thy devotions unto the Most High;
> Nevertheless thy vows shall be offered up in righteousness on all days and at all times;
> But remember that on this, the Lord's day, thou shalt offer thine oblations and thy sacraments unto the Most High, confessing thy sins unto thy brethren, and before the Lord.
> And on this day thou shalt do none other thing, only let thy food be prepared with singleness of heart that thy fasting may be perfect, or, in other words, that thy joy may be full.
> Verily, this is fasting and prayer, or in other words, rejoicing and prayer. (D&C 59:5–14)

All too often our conversations about the Sabbath day—whether at church or home, informally among family and friends, or more formally in talks or lessons in quorums and classes—revolve around discussions about what activities are acceptable on the Sabbath and which ones clearly violate the letter and spirit of the law. In fact, we have found it amusing (and at times somewhat discouraging) to listen to a discussion in a Sunday school class or other setting as the teacher discusses how Jesus condemned the Pharisees and scribes of His day for making their traditional, burdensome lists of acceptable Sabbath observance. Yet within a few moments of class discussion, we ourselves are making lists and debating the merits (or demerits) of certain Sabbath-day activities. It is not uncommon to have debates, even spirited disagreements, over what constitutes "Sabbath appropriate." Are we not like the scribes and Pharisees of Jesus's day when we focus so much on the *whats* (What can we do?) and not so much on the *whys* (Why does the Lord want me to honor His holy day?)? As we have noted, the very essence of the Savior's teachings regarding the Sabbath and His repudiation of the "traditions of the elders" is that holiness cannot be obtained solely through outward observance. Inward faith, devotion, love, and true worship is what gives life and joy to any commandment. Sabbath worship isn't as much about *behavior* as it is about *devotion*.

There is probably no more clear and poignant statement regarding *why* we are invited—even commanded—to "remember the Sabbath day, to keep it holy" than the Lord's statement in this dispensation to the Prophet Joseph Smith: "And that thou mayest more fully keep thyself unspotted from the world." What a great reason to honor the Sabbath. Keeping *it* holy keeps *us* holy.

Devout Jews today identify 613 commandments or *mitzvoth* (laws). Yet despite all the laws—many of which are very behavioral in nature—Jesus taught that "all the Law and the prophets" can be capsulized into the two great commandments: loving God and loving our fellow men (see Matthew 22:36–40). Similarly, all the expectations of "honoring," "keeping," "observing," or "reverencing" the Lord's day can be found in the Savior's simple two-fold admonition: "rest from your labors," and "pay thy devotions unto the Most High" (D&C 59:10). In our day as well as in ancient times, it really boils down to two things: rest and glorify God (see JST, Mark 2:28)—on these two "hang all the law and the prophets."

"Rest from Your Labors"

As a busy stake president, Brent usually thinks the phrase "day of rest" is an oxymoron as it relates to his typical Sundays. And it is not just stake presidents, bishops, Primary presidents, or nursery leaders who may feel that way. Probably all of us at some time or another have felt anything but rested on the Sabbath. There are meetings galore, choir practice, getting the kids ready for church, and hoping the kids will *stay* ready for church. How can a day that is sometimes so stressful and busy be a day of rest? The answer to that question is found in the meaning of *rest*. A real attitude adjustment about the "day of rest" occurs when we come to know how the Lord wants us to "rest."

In the scriptures we are told, "And on the seventh day God ended his work which he had made; and he *rested* on the seventh day from all his work which he had made. And God blessed the seventh day, and sanctified it: because that in it he had *rested* from all his work which God created and made" (Genesis 2:2–3; emphasis added). The Hebrew word from which we get the translated words "rest" and "rested" is *yishbot*. It is built upon the same root as *Shabbat*, which means "stopped" or "ceased."

Did God "rest" in the sense that he was tired from all the "work" of Creation? Does (or can) an omnipotent God even get tired? Does He need to (or just want to) go take a nap in the solitude and beauty of the Garden of Eden? Of course not! Those questions may appear irreverent, but they are not intended that way. They should get us to think about "rest" in a different—even higher—way than we typically do. There is so much more involved in this account. Understanding this higher meaning of "rest" gives deeper meaning and higher purpose to the divine expectation to "rest from your labors" (D&C 59:10).

For centuries there have been theological debates on this subject and these very questions. For example, to the Jews, "rest" and avoiding "work" is viewed very, very literally. There is a distinctly physical dimension involved. To early Christians, the "rest" imposed by a Jewish Sabbath bordered on laziness. Many viewed Sabbath "rest" as merely symbolic—foreshadowing the future "rest" we will enjoy in the glory of God's presence in eternity. Well, which one of those is right? The answer, in our estimation, is that there is a kernel of truth in each of those explanations—and we think there are relevant applications in each to an LDS view of "honoring" the Sabbath day.

Sabbath—the "day of rest"—marked the end of one period and the beginning of another, a transition from "normal time" to "sacred time." It is a "doorway," so to speak—a day that celebrates the end of physical creation and points us to the ultimate spiritual creation in which we become "new creatures in Christ," sanctified and prepared to dwell in the presence of God. Sabbath was given to man to be a time of sanctification—being made whole, complete, finished, holy.

The Sabbath "day of rest" described in Genesis 2 could be compared to the dedication of a temple. After a long period of physical construction—when it is declared "good" or "finished"— there is a day of holy dedication, giving the edifice its rightful honor. It is a time of celebration—"rest," so to speak—but it is also a time of rededicating ourselves to God's work and glory, which the temple represents and facilitates. The temple dedication, like the Sabbath, is a transitional event that marks the end of physical "construction" and opens the door for the spiritual transformation that is the ultimate objective. In other words, God's "work" changes from temporal to spiritual.

So what does this mean to us today? It means much, much more than a nice Sunday afternoon nap. Yes, temporal rest is important, but the "rest" offered by the Sabbath is a spiritual transformation. It is experiencing a portion of God's presence and glory in our lives. It is changing us, strengthening us, making us different than the six-day-a-week natural man. "Six days a week we live under the tyranny of things of space," Rabbi Heschel wrote; "on the Sabbath we try to become attuned to *holiness in time*."[21]

William Wordsworth, the famous British poet of the eighteenth- and nineteenth-century Romantic period, wrote "The World Is Too Much with Us," a poem that characterizes the "tyranny" of worldliness that we encounter six days a week and clearly shows a need for "rest." In it, he writes:

The world is too much with us; late and soon,
Getting and spending, we lay waste our powers:
Little we see in Nature that is ours;
We have given our hearts away, a sordid boon!

---

21 Heschel, *The Sabbath*, 10.

The tyrannical temporal demands of life—working, providing for a family, emotional ups and downs, commuting, technology, soccer practice, school, caring for a home, raising children, relationships— all demand something of us, draining our emotional, financial, and physical resources. Even when we don't invite it, the world and worldliness intrude upon us. It is part of the mortal condition. The Sabbath is that liminal "doorway" whereby we can, at least for a day, close the door on the intrusiveness of worldliness and experience the "rest" of a better, higher, more sanctified world. Six days a week we "get and spend," "lay waste our powers," and "give our hearts away" to lesser things. The Sabbath, if we will allow it, gives us back our hearts and powers.

Presbyterian pastor and author, Ryan McGraw, observed that we may not even recognize how much control the world—work, technology, recreation, social media, etc.—has on our hearts and minds and families until we truly try to keep the Sabbath holy.

> Striving to keep the Sabbath holy may reveal that we are out of shape spiritually. Worldliness, or earthly mindedness, may be the underlying cause. The difficulty of laying aside all unnecessary thoughts, words, works about our worldly employments and recreations for an entire day often uncovers the fact that [we have] loved the world and the things of the world in an inordinate manner. . . . I am convinced that the modern aversion to keeping the Sabbath holy is, in part, a result of improper love for the world and a mistaken view of Christian living. The duties of the Sabbath serve as an irritant, aggravating the worldliness that has crept into the hearts and lives of God's people.[22]

Have you ever noticed in your life how the "cares of the world" intrude into your Sabbath, even when you don't want it? Or have you felt the Sabbath as an intrusion or obstacle to what you feel you "have to get done?" Have you noticed, as we have, how we get unwittingly

[22] Ryan M. McGraw, *The Day of Worship—Reassessing the Christian Life in Light of the Sabbath* (Grand Rapids, MI: Reformation Heritage Books, 2011), 65.

"programmed" to patterns and habits that may not be the kind of "rest" the Lord desires for us on the Sabbath? Take for example technology. Our smartphones, tablets, computers, and televisions can be valuable tools to us, not just six days a week, but even on the Sabbath. They can be means whereby we can feel the Spirit, learn the gospel, and draw closer to the Lord. But "the world is too much with us" sometimes. Do you, like we do, have to fight the urge to periodically see what's trending, check our texts, emails, Facebook and Twitter posts, or shop online? We may start off reading our scriptures on our devices, but it doesn't take long before the tentacles of technology can turn our Sabbath "day of rest" into just another day.

There was an interesting story on a television news program recently. It was a program on addictions and how the brain becomes "programmed." A group of adults were promised $100 to participate in an hour-long focus group. The caveat was that they had to "turn in" their cell phones and not use them during the focus group. They even signed a "contract" stating that they would forfeit the money if they left the meeting or used their devices. Unbeknownst to the participants, it was a test. After gathering up the devices and putting them in a basket on a table in the front of the conference room, researchers would then send messages to or call the numbers of the participants in the group. They could hear the pings or the vibrating, buzzing of the phone in silent mode. Could they ignore the alerts for the hour-long meeting? Remember, a hundred bucks was on the line. Yet, when the leader of the focus group left the room for a moment (all part of the experiment), almost everyone in the room felt the need to check their phones. Some even left the group to text or make calls (none of them were emergencies or pressing needs). They could not go one hour without their technology. This is a great example of how the world intrudes upon us. No wonder our loving Father has given us a day to "rest" from that.

"Resting from [our] labors," as the Lord declared in Doctrine and Covenants 59, therefore, is not just *not working* in our daily employment or responsibilities. If that were the case, then any activity that was not technically "work-related" would constitute "rest." Unfortunately, all too many interpret Sunday "rest" that way, justifying recreation, entertainment, shopping—anything that is not directly related to the workplace. "The word Sabbath properly signifies, not common, but *sacred* or *holy* rest," Thomas Shephard, founder of Harvard University, wrote in 1649.

> The Lord, therefore, enjoins this rest from labor upon this day, not so much for the rest's sake, but because it is a medium, or means that holiness which the Lord requires upon this day; otherwise the Sabbath is a day of idleness, not of holiness; our cattle rest but a common rest from labor as well as we; and therefore it is man's sin and shame if he improve the day no better than the beasts that perish.[23]

According to Jewish philosophy, when God finished the work of creation in six days, he found that something was missing. The universe would not be complete or "good" until there was the Sabbath and the *menuha* it brings.

> *Menuha* which we usually render with "rest" means here much more than withdrawal from labor and exertion, more than freedom from toil, strain or activity of any kind. *Menuha* is not a negative concept but something real and intrinsically positive. This must have been the view of the ancient rabbis if they believe it took a special act of creation [by God] to bring it into being, that the universe would be incomplete without it.
>
> What was created on the seventh day? *Tranquility, serenity, peace,* and *repose.*
>
> To the biblical mind *menuha* is the same as happiness and stillness, as peace and harmony. . . . It is the state wherein man lies still, wherein the wicked cease from troubling and weary are at rest. It is the state in

---

[23] Thomas Shephard, *Theses Sabbaticae* (1649; reprinted Dahlonega, GA: Crown Rights Book Company, 2002), 254.

which there is no strife and no fighting, no fear and no distrust. The essence of good life is *menuha*.[24]

In this manner, God's "creation" of us is incomplete—just like the physical creation of the earth was incomplete until He sanctified it with His presence. Thus, the Sabbath is intended to give us a portion of His presence, His holiness, His "rest." We "rest" on the Sabbath by actions and attitudes that are focused more on eternity than on the tyranny of the here and now. It should be at least a foretaste, even if just a small nibble, of the exquisite joy, peace, and happiness that is found in God's celestial kingdom. In contrast to the profane and mundane of the other days, the Lord's day should be sanctifying. Perhaps as we consider what we should do and think and feel on the Sabbath, we should ask ourselves: Does this reflect God's rest? Does this give us a "taste" of the delight we will feel in His presence? As Abraham Heschel wrote: "Unless one learns how to relish the taste of Sabbath while still in this world, unless one is initiated in the appreciation of eternal life, one will be unable to enjoy the taste of eternity in the world to come. Sad is the lot of him who arrives inexperienced and when led to heaven has no power to perceive the beauty of the Sabbath."[25]

"Pay Thy Devotions unto the Most High"

Not long ago Brent and a few of his colleagues in Religious Education at BYU were invited to make a presentation on the Sabbath to the Church Area Committee. That committee is comprised of the members of the Quorum of the Twelve, the Presidency of the Seventy, and the Presiding Bishopric of the Church. Talk about an intimidating and stressful assignment! The presentation was followed by a question-and-answer session. The presentation was not all that memorable, but the discussion with and among the Brethren was most remarkable. Somehow in the course of the discussion, Brent was asked about the challenges of balancing the need to honor the Sabbath day with the heavy demands of being a stake president. "I spend a lot of time *serving* the Lord, but not as

---

24 Heschel, *The Sabbath*, 22–23.

25 Ibid., 74.

much time *worshipping* Him," he responded. What followed was an insightful discussion and pointed counsel from one of the senior Apostles about not letting the administrative demands of our Church callings crowd out the worship aspect of the Sabbath—"paying [our] devotions unto the Most High." Since that experience, we have thought much about what that phrase means, what we personally can do to increase the spirit of worship on Sunday, and protect against the "crowding out" of essential, even imperative things by other tasks and responsibilities, which, though important and helpful, may actually get in the way of worship. Certainly, serving the Lord and our fellow men by magnifying our Church callings is *one* part of Sabbath worship, but not the *only* part.

On the Sabbath we are to "pay [our] devotions," but what does that mean? "Devotions" is defined as any expressions—attitudinal, behavioral, emotional, verbal, etc.—of love and affection, loyalty, gratitude, faithfulness, commitment, adoration, and worship. Devotion is a state of connectedness. Section 59 in the Doctrine and Covenants uses two unique words in discussing how we "pay" *devotions* in our Sabbath worship—*oblations* and *sacraments*. They are not synonyms. Yet, they are related. Each is an essential part of the sanctifying power of the Sabbath.

Oblations

The word *oblation* means an offering, a gift of gratitude, a token of one's love, an act of worship. The footnote for Doctrine and Covenants 59:12 specifically defines *oblations* as "offerings, whether of time, talents, or means in service of God and fellowman." Thus, the Lord is teaching us that the Sabbath is a day for us to give of our time, talents, and resources to serve God and others. Thus, when we teach a lesson or give a talk, serve as a door greeter, listen attentively and reverently, participate in class and quorum discussion, or any number of other things, we may be "offering [our] oblations." Note we said *may*. Clearly, we are *doing* something. The question, however, is whether we are *giving*—giving from our heart and soul an offering of love, gratitude, and worship.

There is a closely related word—*obligation*. It has both positive and negative connotations, depending upon the context. On the positive side, an *obligation* is "an act or course of action to which a person is morally or legally bound; a duty or commitment." When we make a covenant, we become *obligated* to live that covenant. We have chosen that course and it becomes our duty. Unfortunately, in today's vernacular, the words *obligation, obligate,* and *obliged* are most commonly understood to mean "doing something because we have to," because of some external expectation or requirement. Whatever the definition, the application to the Sabbath is apparent. Some "keep the Sabbath day holy" because they are obligated to do so. Perhaps our children would have fallen into this category as they were growing up in our home. We taught them and expected them to do so. Hopefully they progressed from being obligated to live Sabbath standards just because that was what we did in our home to willingly doing so out of a sense of spiritual duty or in obedience to our covenants as members of the Lord's Church. There are great blessings associated with that. Ultimately, however, the Lord's day becomes holy to us personally—in the truest sense of the word—as our attitudes and observance move from *obligation* to *oblation*— giving the Lord on the Sabbath our own personal offering of love and gratitude to Him—from just *sacrificing* to fully *consecrating*. In this manner, how we live and love the Sabbath becomes our own personal "sign" to the "Lord of the Sabbath." President Russell M. Nelson illustrates this very principle:

> In my much younger years, I studied the work of others who had compiled lists of things to do and things *not* to do on the Sabbath. It wasn't until later that I learned from the scriptures that my conduct and attitude on the Sabbath constituted a *sign* between me and Heavenly Father. With that understanding, I no longer needed lists of dos and don'ts. When I had to make a decision whether or not an activity was appropriate for the Sabbath, I simply asked myself, "What *sign* do I want to give to God?" That question made my choices about the Sabbath day crystal clear.[26]

---

[26] Russell M. Nelson, "The Sabbath Is a Delight," *Ensign*, May 2015, 130.

Sacraments

"Offer up thy sacraments upon my holy day," the Lord declared in Doctrine and Covenants 59:9. It is interesting to note that it doesn't just say "partake of *the* sacrament." Of course, the ordinance of the sacrament of the Lord's Supper is and will always be (at least in mortality) the central focus of the Sabbath, but the scriptural use of *sacraments* plural is significant to an understanding of what constitutes Sabbath *worship*.

While we generally think of "sacraments" as ordinances of salvation (which they certainly are), there is a more general definition. The English word "sacrament" comes from the Latin *sacramentum* which has at its root *sacro*, which means "to consecrate or hallow." In this general sense, that which we consecrate unto the Lord—a holy offering—is a sacrament—a sacred gift of devotion to the Lord (an oblation) which will return to us sanctification and holiness.

So what does this mean to us? What do *sacraments* have to do with "keeping the Sabbath day holy?" Everything. A person can "rest" without sacraments—without giving anything to the Lord, without any activities devoted to religious worship, without any thought of seeking holiness. We call that recreation. Likewise, a person can attend church—even partake of *the* sacrament—without "paying [his/her] devotions unto the Most High." We call that activity. But making the Sabbath a holy day involves much more than just rest and church activity. It requires, as President James E. Faust taught, "spiritual renewal and worship" and "regeneration and the strengthening of our spiritual being." Thus, it is about devotion (internal), not just deeds (external). "Where is the line as to what is acceptable and unacceptable on the Sabbath?" President Faust asked. It is *the* question each of us has asked and been asked numerous times. His answer perhaps captures best the very essence of what it means to "keep the Sabbath day holy."

> Within guidelines, each of us must answer this question for ourselves. While these guidelines are contained in the scriptures and the words of modern prophets, they must be written in our hearts and governed by our conscience. . . . It is quite unlikely that there will

be any serious violation of Sabbath worship if we come humbly before the Lord and offer him all our heart, our soul, and our mind.[27]

Perhaps it would be easier to live the Mosaic law—to have every detail prescribed, every "right" and every "wrong" clearly identified. Perhaps. On the other hand, we should remember why it was called a "lesser law." Higher blessings require a higher law. A higher law demands deeper devotion. Deep devotion requires deep, personal (and family) introspection. Introspection leads to inspiration—the Holy Spirit teaching us where we are on the pathway of devoted discipleship and what course corrections we need to make in our lives. The Sabbath, and particularly the sacred ordinance of the sacrament of the Lord's Supper, is perhaps the greatest means whereby we can do that introspection and receive that instruction. In the next chapter, we will deal specifically with the sacrament—its purposes, blessings, and central role in Sabbath worship.

---

[27] James E. Faust, "The Lord's Day," *Ensign*, November 1991, 34, 36.

CHAPTER 6
"That They May Always Have His Spirit to Be with Them"

DURING OUR MANY TRIPS TO our basement storeroom to retrieve decorations this past Christmas season, we noticed several items that belonged to our deceased parents. There were Brent's father's set of scriptures and his scouting Silver Beaver award and the Purple Heart awarded to Wendy's father in World War II. There were various knick-knacks that our mothers collected and displayed in their homes. There were scrapbooks and photo albums. Each item, along with the photo books that we paused to peruse, brought a flood of memories. It was much more than just a momentary "journey down memory lane."

We were powerfully reminded of how much we loved them, how much they loved us, and all that they had done for us through the years. We could almost hear their voices as we remembered their encouragement, their teachings of important principles, and their expressions of love. We were filled with deep gratitude and love for them. It was so good to have a few quiet moments amidst the hectic holiday season to remember them and reflect on things that matter a great deal to us and our family. We found ourselves wishing that we could just sit down together again with our loved ones and have a deep conversation with them. We wanted and needed their counsel and encouragement again. We wanted to hug and hold them once more. This sentimental and reflective experience made us want to be better *for them* because of what they taught and did for us. We wanted to once again feel their love and their approbation of our efforts to live as we were taught, and we wanted to feel that they were indeed proud of us and they were pleased with their posterity. Perhaps you have had similar experiences and feelings.

Remembering

In the days since, we have thought a great deal about how certain objects and events trigger loving memories and how remembering can be a catalyst to change and increased commitment. That is the purpose of the sacrament of the Lord's Supper. With the breaking of the bread and sharing the cup of wine at His last Passover, Jesus taught the disciples that the bread is in "remembrance of my body which I give a ransom for you" (JST Matthew 26:22) and the wine was "in remembrance of my blood of the new testament, which is shed for as many as shall believe on my name, for the remission of sins" (JST Matthew 26:24). "The sacrament and the partaking of these emblems," President Gordon B. Hinckley declared, "is the *very heart of our Sabbath worship*."[28]

Each Sabbath day as we enter the chapel for sacrament meeting, we observe on a table in the front of the chapel under the clean, white linen cloth (representing a burial shroud) trays of bread and cups of water—representing the broken body and spilled blood of the sacrificial Lamb of God. The sacrament table should engender in us the same feelings of reverence, solemnity, gratitude, and love as standing before the open casket of a departed loved one.

As profound as our experiences were as we remembered our beloved parents, the sacrament can have an infinitely more profound effect on us. As much as we felt love for and from our parents as we beheld those tangible artifacts and photographs, we can feel the Savior's divine love infinitely more when we "partake of His body," figuratively speaking, and "drink of His blood." Yet, we don't always feel that way. Why not?

It may be, at least for us and from our experience, because we "forget" to remember—to remember with a divine remembering that comes from deep within our souls. "Always remembering Him" is easier said than done. It is so easy to become distracted by the pressing demands of life, Sunday responsibilities, or just plain fatigue. We may start out thinking about the Savior during the sacrament hymn. We might even think about Him during the quiet time the sacrament is being passed, but then all too often our minds wander—

---

[28] Gordon B. Hinckley, *Teachings of Gordon B. Hinckley* (Salt Lake City: Deseret Book, 1997), 561.

sometimes not just wander, but actually rush from one thought to the next—some spiritual, some not so much. It may be that we have what we characterize as "spiritual attention deficit disorder." As fallen women and men, we all do. That is the very reason why the Lord has given us that sacred ordinance—that we may regularly remember Him and obtain the blessings that come with "deep remembering." The ordinance of the sacrament of the Lord's Supper is the means whereby we can be cured of "spiritual ADD." We covenant to "always remember Him" (D&C 20:77, 79)—not just during those moments when the emblems of the Savior's Atonement are blessed and passed and consumed—but "at all times and in all things, and in all places" (Mosiah 18:9).

The sacrament provides us with a regular, quiet, sacred space in which we can introspectively search our souls, our hearts, and our lives. It is the means whereby we can "remember to remember" the Savior. With that sacred intent of this holy ordinance—which, as Elder Jeffrey R. Holland taught, "comes to us more readily and more repeatedly than any other in our life in what has been called the 'most sacred, the most holy of all the meetings of the Church'"[29]—what, then, can we remember?

We can remember that Jesus went "forth, suffering pains and afflictions and temptations of every kind . . . that he might blot out [our] transgressions" (Alma 7:11, 13). We can remember that He is "mighty to save" (Alma 34:18) and that because of His perfect love, we are encircled in His "arms of safety" (Alma 34:16). Deep remembering of Him reminds us of His deep remembering of us.

We can remember that, unless we are under a priesthood leader-imposed restriction from partaking of the sacrament or we have no desire to repent, change, and strive to do better, we are worthy to partake of the sacrament. The sacrament is for sinners who are striving to be Saints. The sacrament is for those who have, during the week, made mistakes, had bad thoughts, or said cross or crass words, done dumb things, and disappointed others. The sacrament is for the weak—for those who have fallen down and fallen short, but who

---

[29] Jeffrey R. Holland, "This Do in Remembrance of Me," *Ensign*, November 1995, 67–68; also included in Elder Holland's statement is a quote from Joseph Fielding Smith, *Doctrines of Salvation*, 2:340.

want to get up, get going, and do and be better. We can—we must—remember that.

We can remember those times when our sins have been forgiven and we have felt peace of conscience. We can gratefully acknowledge the goodness of God and the cleansing power of Christ's Atonement. We can long to "retain a remission of [our] sins" and remember that partaking of the sacrament and striving to keep our covenants will bring that.

We can remember the promise "that they may *always* have his Spirit to be with them." We can remember what it is like to have the Spirit strengthen us in adversity and temptation, comfort us in sorrow or loneliness, teach us things we did not know or may have forgotten, and guide us when we don't know what to do or where to go. We can remember the still, small voice. We can gratefully acknowledge the blessing of the gift of the Holy Ghost.

Repenting

In the Old Testament, the Hebrew word that is translated in our English scriptures as *repentance* is *shuv.* It means "to turn"—to turn *from* sin and turn *to* God. As we *turn* our hearts and minds to the Savior during the sacrament, we can also *turn* our thoughts to our imperfections—those thoughts and actions during the past week that have placed spiritual wedges in our relationship with the Lord. While we should be in a continual state of repentance—striving to turn from the ways of the "natural man" and becoming "a saint through the atonement of Christ the Lord" (Mosiah 3:19)—the sacrament and sacrament meeting provide us with important means to do that.

During the administration of the sacrament, we can pray to know what things we need to turn from and what things must be done to put us on the right path. Of course, we do not believe that partaking of the sacrament is *all* that needs to be done to repent, but it is certainly a valuable resource in the repentance process. Often our singing of sacrament hymns and pondering and praying as the emblems of the Lord's sacrifice are being prepared by the priests and passed to the congregation by the deacons serve as catalysts to deeper repentance. Partaking of those emblems becomes tangible, albeit symbolic, tokens of our broken heart and contrite spirit—our deepest desires to turn from all evil and return to righteousness. Eating the blessed bread and water—symbols of the Savior's suffering for us—should be a powerful catalyst to change. Sometimes partaking of the sacrament is the culmination of a repentance process—an acknowledgment that, with the Lord's grace, we are on the path again. The road of repentance always intersects with the sacrament of the Lord's Supper.

Renewing

In addition to being a time of remembering and repenting, the sacrament is a time of renewing—renewing our covenants, renewing our determination to serve the Lord and keep His commandments (see 2 Nephi 31:12–20; Mosiah 18:10; Moroni 6:2–3; D&C 20:37). Many leaders of the Church in this dispensation have taught that partaking of the sacrament is a time of renewal of covenants. Brigham Young taught that "the bread and cup [are for] a renewal of their covenants."

In *The Articles of Faith*, Elder James E. Talmage wrote, "Partaking of the sacrament worthily may be regarded . . . as a means of *renewing our avowals before the Lord*." Elder Delbert L. Stapley taught in 1956 that "another important purpose of the sacrament is to *renew and keep in force* the covenants and obligations which we have entered into with our God." Likewise, President Ezra Taft Benson declared, "We go to our chapels each week to worship the Lord and renew our covenants by partaking of the sacrament." President Gordon B. Hinckley said, "As we partake of the sacrament we all stand on a level plane before the Lord. Each is accountable for what he does as he renews his covenants with the Lord in that magnificent and beautiful and simple ordinance of the gospel."[30]

This concept of the sacrament as a time of *renewing* was addressed recently as well. Elder Neil L. Andersen observed that the term *renewing our covenants* "is not found in the scriptures. [But] it is not inappropriate."

---

[30] *Teachings of Gordon B. Hinckley*, 561; see also "I Have a Question—What covenants do we renew when we partake of the sacrament? Response by John E. MacKay," *Ensign*, March 1995, and "Visiting Teaching Message—Renewing Covenants through the Sacrament," *Liahona*, June 2010.

In the April 2015 General Conference Training Meeting for General Auxiliary Presidencies, General Authorities, and Area Seventies, Elder Andersen taught:

> Spirituality is not stagnant and neither are covenants. And hopefully, we pray that all of us as members are moving along a progressive growth in our spirituality and in our covenants. Covenants bring not only commitments, but they bring spiritual power. We should teach our members that we are moving towards our Heavenly Father. The sacrament is a beautiful time to not just renew our baptismal covenants, but to commit to Him to renew all our covenants, all our promises, and to approach Him in a spiritual power that we did not have as we move forward.[31]

When we presided over the Illinois Peoria Mission several years ago, we taught the missionaries about the importance of dedications and rededications. We explained that countries and missions are "opened" for the preaching of the gospel with a dedicatory prayer. The Holy Land was "dedicated" by Orson Hyde for the purpose of gathering and blessing the children of Father Abraham. Likewise, temples and other meetinghouses of worship in the Church are "dedicated" unto the Lord. Even our homes can and should be "dedicated." Sometimes, they are "rededicated."

A *rededication* doesn't mean that the original dedication "didn't take" or that something went terribly wrong. It is just as the word indicates: it is a *rededication*—a renewal of prayers and promises and a renewed commitment to bringing about the purposes of God. In a way, it is like our personal and family prayers. We "renew" our expressions of gratitude and petitions to our Father in Heaven for His blessings.

President Top explained to the missionaries that the mission had been dedicated and rededicated (in fact, rededicated several times). He encouraged them, as companionships and leaders of

---

31 Neil L. Andersen, General Conference Training Meeting, April 2015; www.lds. org/broadcasts/archive/general-conference-leadership-training/2015/04?lang=eng

the mission, to offer a prayer of *rededication* in their own areas. He further explained that such a formal prayer and priesthood blessing, as important as it is in and of itself, was really an *outward* expression of the missionaries' *inward* recommitment to the Lord and His work. A missionary's prayer by itself—even the pronounced priesthood blessing on the area—would not bring about a hastening of the work and increased conversions without a *personal rededication*—a renewing of one's own commitment to love, serve, obey, and work.

In the early days of the Church in this dispensation, particularly after the Saints arrived in the Salt Lake Valley, baptized members of the Church were rebaptized as a sign of renewal and rededication. This went on for many years, until finally the leadership of the Church put an end to the practice because it was an unnecessary act of recommitment. There was already in place the proper procedure for renewal and rededication—the partaking of the sacrament of the Lord's Supper.

Many years ago when our oldest daughter was baptized, a member of our extended family called Jessica to congratulate her on her baptism. "I wish I could be rebaptized," this family member casually said to our daughter, probably not even realizing the significance of what she was saying. This family member had not been active in the Church for many, many years. The statement was not lost on us. In fact, we hoped that the family member felt the Spirit and would be inspired in some way to re-engage with the Church. We have thought about that moment and wished we had said something like, "You don't have to be rebaptized. All you have to do is come back to church and partake of the sacrament."

A broken piece of bread and cup of water—blessed by priesthood power—partaken of by one with clean hands and pure heart is a formal, public ritual, an outward ordinance of renewal. But spiritual renewal occurs only with personal inward rededication—renewing one's own dedication to the Lord and determination to follow in His steps.

Receiving

Every one of us, after we were baptized, had hands laid upon our heads and were confirmed members of The Church of Jesus Christ of Latter-day Saints. We were commanded to "receive the Holy Ghost." With that holy ordinance, the door was opened to each of us to receive the blessings that come with that sacred companionship. As we partake of the sacrament, the door is once again swung open to us. The commandment is the same—"receive the Holy Ghost"—the promised blessing is renewed "that they may always have His spirit to be with them."

What does that mean? What do we receive? What difference can that sacramental promise make in our lives? As we remember, repent, and renew, we can receive these and numerous other very real blessings through the sacrament:

- A remission of our sins
- Spiritual guidance and direction for our lives
- Comfort
- Healing
- Perspective
- Pure love
- Strength to resist temptation and face the challenges of a fallen world

How grateful we are for the sacred ordinance of the sacrament of the Lord's Supper. It is the crown jewel of the Sabbath—the Lord's day. "In the context of a proper Sabbath, the sacrament draws us to the Atonement of Jesus Christ and its sanctifying power," Elder D. Todd Christofferson testified. "It reconnects us to and reinforces all our covenants with God. It refreshes and renews the promise of the companionship of the Holy Spirit always to be with us."[32]

What an incredible blessing it is to participate in that ordinance regularly and often. Do you, like we, feel the difference in our lives when we miss even a week? There is power in thoughtful, worthy partaking of the sacrament. No wonder the First Presidency and Quorum of the Twelve and other General Authorities who have so many responsibilities and attend so many conferences throughout the world partake of the sacrament every Thursday in the Salt Lake Temple—without fail. That way, they never need miss because of

---

[32] D. Todd Christofferson, General Conference Training Meeting, October 2015; www.lds.org/broadcasts/archive/general-conference-leadership-training/2015/10?lang=eng

hectic travel schedules on the weekends. We have been blessed by the sacrament, by experiencing its benefits in our own lives, and by observing what it does for others.

"To Make Our Hearts as One"

Many years ago when Brent served as a young bishop, he received a phone call late on a Saturday night from a member of the ward. "Bishop, my wife really needs to talk to you," the husband said. He made arrangements to meet them at the bishop's office first thing in the morning. The next day they arrived at the meetinghouse hand in hand, but eyes swollen and red from a night of crying. It seemed like eternity before the wife was able to speak.

When the words finally came, they flowed like a river that had just burst a dam. She had carried the burden of a serious moral transgression for many years. Hiding her transgressions from her husband and priesthood leaders, she continued to live a lie— attending the temple unworthily and serving in the Church as if nothing had ever happened. In the years since her transgressions, she had tried so hard to be as Christlike as she could. "I cannot carry this burden and live this lie any longer," she cried. "I know that I will probably have to be excommunicated," she sobbed, "but I cannot go on like this one more day." Her heart was broken and her spirit contrite. She sobbed about the pain she had caused her husband. Yet he loved her so much and so desired her to be made spiritually whole that it was he who called and lovingly took her by the hand to the bishop's office.

Brent tried to explain to her that excommunication may not be the outcome, but he would need to seek the inspiration of the Lord in knowing how to proceed. They knelt together in prayer as Brent pleaded with the Lord to let him know what would be best for this good woman. As bishop, he was fully prepared to hold a disciplinary council, and it was likely that her membership in the Church would be affected. But during the prayer a remarkable thing occurred. There were no words or angelic beings—just a strong impression to the bishop. He knew the will of God and knew what He would have him say and do.

It was revealed to Brent that this woman had carried a

tremendous burden of guilt through the years, yet had diligently sought to serve the Lord and emulate the Savior in every way possible. He came to know that this confession was the fulfillment of her repentance, not the beginning. There was no need to hold a disciplinary council. Again the tears flowed freely—tears of gratitude and love.

Bishop Top then proceeded to give her some counsel. He told her that ordinarily he would ask her not to partake of the sacrament, but the Spirit had directed him to counsel her to partake of the sacred emblems that day and think deeply of what the Savior had done for her. He promised that her burden would be lifted and that she would indeed experience a spiritual healing.

During the meeting, as the sacrament hymn was sung, Brent couldn't take his eyes off her. It was almost as if he could see into her spirit and witness firsthand what was going on in her soul. He could see that there was more meaning in the words of the hymn to her than to the rest of the congregation. After the sacramental prayer was offered, there was the usual reverence in the chapel as the sacrament was passed, but she possessed a depth of "deep remembering" that, at least for that moment, was unsurpassed in the chapel. When she partook of the bread, Brent saw her bury her head in the shoulder of her husband. He could see her body shudder as she wept. She wept almost uncontrollably. The feelings were deep and personal. The tears were of joy. Brent could almost see the burden being lifted. The miracle of forgiveness and healing was as tangible and real as a physical healing or raising the dead. It was overwhelming to witness this miracle. Never before had the sacrament meant so much.

In the years since that event, we have thought of it many times and have witnessed similar scenes of healing and rededication resulting from the renewal of covenants made possible through worthily partaking of the sacrament. Each of us is like this woman— though our sins and circumstances may be quite different. Yet, we are all "lost and fallen" and totally dependent upon the Savior for His grace, His healing, His power. When we "deeply remember" that, it's unimaginable that anyone would purposely avoid attending sacrament meeting where that holy, healing ordinance is offered to us. When we understand the meaning of the sacrament, we can't imagine texting or talking, socializing or sleeping, daydreaming or doodling during the sacred time. It's too important to trivialize in any way. It is a matter of life and death—becoming "dead" to sin and becoming "alive in Christ" again.

We have been commanded to come to the sacrament table each week with a broken heart and a contrite spirit—with a desire to be better and try harder. As we truly worship the Lord in reverence, love, and gratitude—"deeply remembering Him," not just casually or with "spiritual ADD"—sins will be forgiven, emotional wounds healed, relationships repaired, and lives filled with greater peace and fulfillment. Of this we bear witness.

> That sacred, holy offering
> By man, least understood,
> To have our sins remitted
> And take his flesh and blood,
> That we may ever witness
> The suffering of thy Son,
> And always have his Spirit
> To make our hearts as one.

CHAPTER 7
It's Not about You

SERVING A FULL-TIME MISSION CAN be (and usually is) quite a shock to the system. "This is a lot harder than I expected," was a common observation when we interviewed and interacted with our missionaries in Illinois. Most all of them had long looked forward to and prepared for missionary service. They were generally quite committed to their mission. Nevertheless, it was hard at times. It required more effort and consecration than they anticipated. More than once a missionary expressed the desire to return home—to return to familiar surroundings and routine and to activities that were less demanding and more enjoyable (at least in that missionary's mind). "This just isn't fun," one missionary matter-of-factly stated to President Top as he asked to return home.

"Fun? Is that why you came on a mission?" Brent asked the young elder. "A mission is not about fun. It's about serving the Lord and sharing the blessings of the gospel with others. Fun and enjoyment are not the reason why you serve, but fun, friendships, enjoyment, love, and laughter all come *as you serve for the right reason.* Fun and obedience, hard work and enjoyment, missionary work and happiness are not mutually exclusive."

Teaching this concept to the missionaries was an ongoing challenge. It was time for a "refresher course" when we had heard (more than we cared to) statements like these, often more than once: "Why can't we do it this way?" "My companion bugs me! I want a transfer." "I don't like this place." "Why do we have to follow that rule?" "I'm a 'spirit of the law' missionary, not a 'letter of the law' missionary."

In zone conferences and in other settings, Sister Top would often bluntly tell the missionaries: "It's not about you! It is *all* about the Lord. It is about serving Him out of love and gratitude for His grace and mercy. It's about making His will your will. It's about those you serve. It's about learning to love others more. It's about helping them know the Lord. It's not about you."

In this day and age of "rugged individualism" and emphasis on "personal fulfillment" and "comfort zones," the phrase "It's not about you" could be viewed as painful speech (okay, maybe we are exaggerating). The concept that there is a higher purpose for life in general, and our own individual actions in particular, besides just fun, fulfillment, and self goes against the grain of the world and the natural man. Self-absorption is antithetical to the gospel of Jesus Christ. Our missionaries, like all of us, know that in their heads, but when responsibilities and restrictions bump up against us and disrupt our "comfort zones," we don't like it.

It was interesting to watch those missionaries that really got it—those who loved and served because they knew it was "all about the Lord." They seemed to have more fun, make more friends, have more meaningful relationships, and have deeper spiritual experiences. They emotionally and spiritually matured and developed Christlike attributes. They gained skills and found talents and abilities that they didn't know they had. In contrast, those who were biding their time in the rut of "It's all about me" had less fun and fulfillment, felt less love and more self-pity. Their missions were anything but filled with joy and delight—only drudgery.

There is an interesting concept found in the scriptures that has been called the "principle of indirection"—doing a thing in one direction may result in blessings coming from a different direction. An example is found in the Savior's Sermon on the Mount: "Blessed are the merciful: for they shall obtain mercy" (Matthew 5:7). You extend mercy to others, then God gives mercy to you. Another example is the Lord's teachings that forgiving others is directly related to our own forgiveness (see Matthew 6:12, 18:21–35; D&C 64:7–11).

There are numerous other examples of how blessings flow into the lives of the faithful *indirectly*. Like a boomerang, it starts out going one direction and comes back to you from another. In the lives of faithful disciples, we see how their focus is on serving the Lord and blessing others, but they personally become magnified and fulfilled in ways they had not specifically sought. So it was with our missionaries. Even though, as Sister Top reminded them, "it's not about you," it became about them as blessings flowed into their lives. As Jesus said, "losing" your life in His service results in you "finding" yourself and so much more (see Matthew 10:39).

It works the same way with the Sabbath. "It's not about you." It is the Lord's day, not ours. We are to honor and reverence and "keep" His day. He isn't giving the day to us to do whatever we want—because it's not our day. Yet by "giving back" the day to Him, He gives to us and our families far more than we could obtain or create on "our own day." Of this Isaiah declared:

> If thou turn away thy foot from the Sabbath *from doing thy pleasure* on my holy day; and call the Sabbath a delight, the holy of the Lord, honourable; and shalt honour him, *not doing thine own ways, nor finding thine own pleasure, nor speaking thine own words.*
>
> Then shalt thou delight thyself in the Lord; and I will cause thee to ride upon the high places of the earth, and feed thee with the heritage of Jacob thy father: for the mouth of the Lord hath spoken it. (Isaiah 58:13–14; emphasis added)

It is interesting to note the "if/then" clause of that passage. *If* you "celebrate" His day in His way, *then* His day becomes your delight—as President Gordon B. Hinckley testified, "a blessing without peer."[33] Said another way: Sacrifice something you *want*, then God will give you something you *really want*. Like fasting, we honor the Lord and "keep" His day by giving up some things we desire. In return, the Lord gives us something greater—blessings we really want and need in our lives. Unfortunately, since we don't always see what blessings are in store, we may be unwilling to make the sacrifice. Whether of food or time, money or favorite activities, or a broken heart and contrite

---

33 Gordon B. Hinckley, *Teachings of Gordon B. Hinckley*, 561.

spirit—sacrifice always is an act of faith. It is a "sign" of our faith. And as we often sing, "Sacrifice brings forth the blessings of heaven" (*Hymns*, 27).

Begin with the End in Mind

There are many good and honorable things that one may do on Sunday, but the blessings of the Sabbath are not linked to merely doing good things, but, rather, doing "God things." Pastor Ryan McGraw wrote, "The question we ought to be asking about recreation or any other activity on the Sabbath day is not '*What's wrong with it?*' but rather '*How does it promote the purposes of the day?*'"

> In the simplest terms, we violate the Sabbath by doing what we please on it, rather than what pleases God. Did you notice that each of the prohibitions in [Isaiah 58:13] begins with the phrase "thine own?" *Thine own* ways, *thine own* pleasure, *thine own* words are implicitly contrasted with *God's* ways, *God's* pleasures, and words that please *God*. The Sabbath is *God's* holy day, not *ours*. It is not a day in which we determine what activities please us on our "day off." We must always ask the question, "What pleased God on a day set apart to worship Him?" It is not sufficient to ask, "What is pleasing to God in general?" but rather "What is pleasing to God on this day?" . . . If you view the purpose of the Sabbath as a "holy day" of worship, then you will understand "thine own pleasures" as those not suited to the purposes of the day, no matter how appropriate and lawful they are on the other six days.[34]

Many years ago, when Brent served as a leader in the Young Men auxiliary, the weekly activities planned for the boys were to meet a "priesthood purpose." There were several different dimensions of that primary purpose that were to guide YM leaders and the presidencies of the Aaronic Priesthood quorums as they planned activities. The intent was to identify the specific purpose, *then* plan activities that

---

[34] Ryan M. McGraw, *The Day of Worship*, 50–51.

would help the young men achieve the stated objective. All too often, however, the boys and their leaders (Brent included) would have a favorite activity they wanted to do, then they "found" a priesthood purpose that could "fit"—even if only peripherally. For example, they would play basketball in the cultural hall and call it "building quorum brotherhood."

In these cases, the tail (the activity) was wagging the dog (the purpose). We are quite certain that was not the planning process that the general leaders of the Church—including prophets, seers, and revelators—had in mind.

Unfortunately, we have been guilty of doing the same thing at times with our own Sabbath observance. We hold on tight to some of our favorite activities that we don't want to sacrifice on Sunday, then try to make them "fit" the purpose of the Sabbath. Instead, we should keep focused on the Lord's stated purpose for *His day* and choose those things on *His day* that meet that purpose and bring about what He desires for us on *His day*.

We have always been impressed with a story about how Michelangelo's incredible sculpture masterpieces were created. His "secret" was, he said (we don't know for sure if he really said it or if this is apocryphal, but we like the message), "I see the finished work in the stone and then carve away those things that don't belong." That is an interesting thought. Do we "see" what the Lord wants us to think and feel and do and why He desires that for us? When the "vision" of that divine purpose and the accompanying blessings becomes clear to us, it becomes easy to "carve away" those things that don't belong.

It's Not Just about Family

Not long ago, an interfaith conference was held at Brigham Young University where religious scholars and leaders of many different Christian denominations gave presentations about their own faith traditions. In the Q&A after one of the presentations, a major Evangelical leader was asked what he admired most about the Latter-day Saints and what he wished he could change about them. "Their emphasis on families," he quickly responded. Interestingly, that which he would change was also the LDS emphasis on families.

He characterized it as overemphasis on "forever families," at the expense of emphasis on Christ. "I wish they would talk a little less about family and more about Christ," he stated. In his estimation, the Mormon view of eternal families was both a strength and a weakness.

We were somewhat taken aback by his observation. He didn't understand what seemed perfectly clear to us. There can be no eternal families without Christ. There is no eternal life, no eternal marriage, no "forever families" except through His infinite Atonement and the ordinances and principles of His gospel. And it isn't just in eternity. Christ is the center of a gospel-focused, happy LDS home. "Happiness in family life is most likely achieved when founded upon the teachings of the Lord Jesus Christ." The proclamation from which that statement comes is often prominently displayed in Mormon homes.

Since that interfaith conference, we have pondered much about the relationship of Christ to eternal families. And that has led us once again to the Sabbath. Certainly, family plays a significant role in faithful Sabbath observance, but it is not just a family day. It is a day whereby our families are not just drawn together in greater love and devotion but drawn together to the Lord. As Elder Dallin H. Oaks has taught, sometimes our strengths can become weaknesses.[35] And so it can be with the Sabbath. Family time on the Sabbath can be either a strength or a weakness. Savior-focused family Sabbath worship and activities are strengths. Family-focused Sabbath without clear focus on Him is a weakness. It may enhance our relationships in life, but family togetherness that is centered on worshipping and following the Savior lasts for time *and* eternity.

In 1980, the Church implemented the consolidated meeting schedule. The First Presidency stated that "the purpose of the consolidated meeting schedule is 1) to reemphasize personal and family responsibility for learning, living, and teaching the gospel and 2) to allow Church members more time for personal gospel study, for service to others, and for meaningful activities." The meeting schedule was to allow more time for "home-centered Sabbath activities" whereby the Latter-day Saint home becomes a place where family members "love to be, where they can enrich their lives and

---

[35] See Dallin H. Oaks, "Our Strengths Can Become Our Downfall," *Ensign,* October 1994.

find mutual love, support, appreciation and encouragement."[36] Even with these clear statements of purpose, members of the Church have had to be reminded, even chastened, at times. In 1993, the First Presidency sensed that "many Latter-day Saints have become lax in their observance of the Sabbath day."

> We urge all Latter-day Saints to set this holy day apart from the activities of the world and consecrate themselves by entering into a spirit of worship, thanksgiving, service, and *family-centered activities appropriate to the Sabbath*. As Church members endeavor to make their Sabbath activities compatible with the intent and Spirit of the Lord, their lives will be filled with joy and peace.[37]

Sunday Best

When we were growing up, we heard the phrase "Sunday best" much more than we do today. Usually, it was in reference to clothing, but it was not uncommon to also hear our mothers talk about "Sunday dinner." Both implied "best" or "special"—best clothes for church attendance and best family meal of the week. Sunday best, whether it be in appearance, activities, or attitudes, was in those days an outward acknowledgment that Sunday was truly a special day, different from other days.

In some circles within contemporary Christianity, there have been calls for a return to the "Sunday best" traditions of the past. Others, however, resist it—thinking it puts too much emphasis on appearances rather than what's in the heart. Yet, many bemoan the fact that there is increasing casualness in society, not just with regard to Sabbath worship, but in all aspects of life. The damaging effects of such casualness are seen all around us—particularly when it comes to Sabbath observance. Elder D. Todd Christofferson linked the loss of "Sunday best" to the decline of a "sense of the sacred." Although Elder Christofferson was specifically addressing the concept of

---

36 "News of the Church—Church Consolidates Meeting Schedules," *Ensign*, March 1980.

37 First Presidency (Ezra Taft Benson, Gordon B. Hinckley, Thomas S. Monson), "First Presidency Statement on the Sabbath," *Ensign*, January 1993.

clothing and appearance, his words have a much broader application and deep meaning.

> Some say dress and hair don't matter—they say it's what's inside that counts.
>
> I believe that it is what's inside that truly counts, but that's what worries me. [Casualness] is a message about what is inside a person. It may be pride or rebellion or something else, but at a minimum it says, "I don't get it. I don't understand the difference between the sacred and the profane."
>
> In that condition people are easily drawn away from the Lord. They do not appreciate the value of what they have. I worry about them. Unless they can gain some understanding and capture some feeling for sacred things, they are at risk of eventually losing all that matters most.[38]

It is not our purpose in this book to discuss what constitutes "Sunday best" as it relates to clothing. Neither are we going to deal with the issue of whether a person should stay in church clothes all day on the Sabbath. Nor are we going to wade into the quicksand regarding the merits or appropriateness of fixing a fancy Sunday dinner for the whole family, complete with the nice china, or whether you can use paper plates as you eat your boxed macaroni and cheese. Those are personal, family decisions. So many things factor into those kinds of decisions, not the least of which must be the Spirit. What we *are* emphasizing is "giving our Sunday best"—because of whose day it really is.

In ancient times, Israelites were expected to offer the very best of their flocks and fields as sacrifices unto the Lord. The sacrificial lamb was to be "without blemish." Other offerings had to be the "cream of the crop." Nothing was too good for the Lord. That is the spirit of "Sunday best." It's not about china or fancy meals. It is not about suits and ties or Sunday dresses. It's about *what* we love. It's about *who* we love. It's not about us. It's about Him. Having His presence in our hearts and our homes is worth our "Sunday best."

[38] D. Todd Christofferson, "A Sense of the Sacred," Church Educational System broadcast, November 7, 2004; published in the *New Era*, June 2006.

CHAPTER 8
The Fulness of the Earth Is Yours

FEW COMMANDMENTS IN THE SCRIPTURES are accompanied with such beautifully elaborated blessings as those associated with the commandment to keep the Sabbath day holy. In Doctrine and Covenants 59 and Isaiah 58, the keeping of the Sabbath day is also closely linked to fasting, perhaps because both require a very personal, individual sacrifice, and the purposes of both center around healing, forgiving, relieving, and drawing nearer to God (see Isaiah 58:6–7; D&C 59:13–14). Moreover, just as the Sabbath is the end result of the Creation, the enjoyment and employment of the Creation—even to the point of inheriting the earth—is one of the rewards of fasting and observing the Sabbath.

Yet, as we hope we have made clear throughout this book, these same chapters in the scriptures clarify that going through the motions is not enough to qualify us for these blessings. Speaking of fasting, Isaiah mockingly asks those who wanted credit from God for their showy sacrifice, "Wherefore have we fasted, say they, and thou seest not? wherefore have we afflicted our soul, and thou takest no knowledge?" (Isaiah 58:3). In Doctrine and Covenants 59, the Lord noted that the blessings will come only "inasmuch as ye do these things with thanksgiving, with cheerful hearts and countenances" (D&C 59:15)—all of which signify inward commitment. With these qualifications, eternal abundance awaits us.

Blessings Promised in Isaiah's Day

In Isaiah 58, there are only two verses that specifically address the Sabbath. However, faith-filled fasting, mentioned in the first twelve verses, and faith-filled observance of the Sabbath seem to go hand in hand. As we have suggested, we can especially appreciate this in our day when we hold our "official" fast day on the Sabbath.

We previously examined Isaiah 58:13, in which Isaiah importunes us to make the Sabbath a delight. The Hebrew word *oneg* or *anag* (vowels are negotiable when transliterating from Hebrew to the Roman alphabet) used in this verse and the next verse comes from a root word meaning "daintiness, or exquisite pleasure." What could daintiness possibly have to do with the way we observe the Sabbath? One of the definitions of the noun *dainty* is "a delicacy." At the time of the King James translators, the word *dainty* had come from Anglo-French and also implied "worthiness" and "happiness"[39]—an interesting combination. Indeed, the word *delight* itself is also defined as having "a high degree of pleasure or enjoyment; joy; rapture" and is originally derived from the Latin for "delectable."[40]

Delight, delicacy, delectable—perhaps Isaiah is intimating that we should relish the Sabbath like an exquisite delicacy that only the worthy or those who live on a higher spiritual plane can appreciate. It is a delicious morsel from heaven. He declares that if we will make the Sabbath a delight, "Then shalt thou *delight* thyself in the Lord; and I will cause thee to ride upon the high places of the earth, and feed thee with the heritage of Jacob thy father" (Isaiah 58:14; emphasis added). These simple phrases encompass the richest blessings the Lord has to offer, available only to those willing to pay the price. Perhaps you and your family could set aside some time on a Sabbath to discuss what this passage means to you. In the meantime, let us share with you a few ideas and insights we have found especially meaningful.

"Then Shalt Thou Delight Thyself in the Lord"

As we previously discussed, King James translators sought to convey a high degree of joy and satisfaction with the word *delight*. Further, Isaiah apparently used the same word, *oneg*, for both delighting in the Sabbath and the delighting in the Lord that would result, thereby closely linking our efforts to keep the Sabbath day

---

[39] www.dictionary.com/browse/dainty, accessed June 1, 2016.

[40] www.dictionary.com/browse/delight?s=t, accessed June 1, 2016.

integral to our relationship with the Lord. Perhaps this is another example of the law of indirection—blessed are those who have exquisite pleasure in the Sabbath, for they will also have exquisite pleasure in their relationship with the Lord, and vice versa.

As mentioned, the blessings of the fast are entwined with the blessings of the Sabbath in the scriptures. One particular blessing identified by Isaiah in verses 8 and 9 of chapter 58 comes to mind here as we contemplate an exquisite joy in the Lord: "Thy righteousness shall go before thee; the glory of the Lord shall be thy rearward. Then shalt thou call, and the Lord shall answer; thou shalt cry, and he shall say, Here I am."

Some have also equated the phrase "delight thyself in the Lord" with the phrase "then shall thy confidence wax strong in the presence of God" (see D&C 121:45), revealed to Joseph Smith as he agonized through the indignities of Liberty Jail. Certainly, when we have reached a place where we genuinely try to keep the Sabbath sacred, it implies that we enjoy a greater righteousness wherein we can go to the Lord with confidence in time of need and call down His aid and blessing upon us. All of these imply a close relationship with the Lord, even a oneness and a mutual adoration.

"I Will Cause Thee to Ride upon the High Places of the Earth"

In ancient times, especially in the land of Israel, "the high places of the earth" had several related connotations. Israel is a country of mountains and valleys. Those who controlled the fortified high places also ruled the valleys. That included the farmland and important travel and trade routes. Kings lived in walled cities on the tops of mountains where they commanded armies that protected them. They could see the enemy coming from afar. This meant they could prepare and fight from a position of great advantage. For those who had farms and vineyards outside the city, safety was found inside the walled cities on the mountaintops. Away from the cities, wealthy landowners held the high places where they could build watchtowers to overlook their possessions and protect them from enemies. High places were associated with power, safety, and dominion as well as prosperity and abundance.

High places were also considered places of sacrifice, worship, holiness, and communion with God. While many of these high places were dedicated to pagan gods, the children of Israel also used them when they had no temple. Consider Mount Moriah, where Abraham attempted to sacrifice Isaac in obedience to the Lord's commandment and where an angel appeared and other possible temple-related activities subsequently took place (see Genesis 15). This holy high altar later became the location of Solomon's and later Herod's temples. Melchizedek, King of Salem, Prince of Peace, presided and sanctified his people there until, like Enoch's Zion, they were taken into heaven. Faithful Israelites arguably would have associated "high places" with the blessings of the temple, including revelation and sanctification as well as worship and communion with Deity. "High places" were places where heaven and earth intersected—places where the Lord met His people.

In our modern vernacular, we have similar phrases that convey similar feelings or ideas. We could use phrases like being "on top of the world," "living the high life," having "friends in high places," or being "above the fray." Each of these sayings implies an elevated life, a way of happiness, prosperity, abundance, or power. They suggest that one is not being a helpless victim of life or bumbling haplessly through it, but rather having dominion over it, having influence over others, making positive choices, overcoming obstacles, and even having abundance of the things of the earth.

Yet riding on the high places of the earth does not always mean riches and power in a temporal sense, though that may be the case in some instances. We have heard stories of those who owned businesses but refused to open them on Sunday, and who have been so blessed. And yet there are many who don't observe the Sabbath who also have power and riches, so it must be something infinitely greater.

Those who keep the Sabbath holy feel blessed with riches and abundance of the kind that really matters to them. They have assurance that they will be cared for temporally and spiritually. Again, from those verses containing the blessings of a worthy fast: "And the Lord shall guide thee continually, and satisfy thy soul in drought, and make fat thy bones: and thou shalt be like a watered garden, and like a spring of water, whose waters fail not" (v. 11). The greatest blessings are those of a spiritual nature—those that bring us peace and contentment with our lives, that give us power to face our challenges, that bless our families and our nation and keep us safe from evil, that prepare us for eternal life, that give us a taste of life in the presence of God the Father and Jesus Christ.

"And Feed Thee with the Heritage of Jacob Thy Father"

The heritage of Jacob refers to the covenant blessings of a promised land, a promised priesthood, and a promised posterity given to Abraham, Isaac, and Jacob for their faithful covenant keeping. Today we receive these same promises in the ordinances of the temple.

In many ways, this expression could be considered a parallel phrase to the first promise, for the temple is the ultimate high place of the earth. We could further summarize and clarify both phrases with still another scripture. Being fed "with the heritage of Jacob," along with riding "upon the high places of the earth," could both finally be equated with "Blessed are the meek: for they shall inherit the earth" (Matthew 5:5)—inheriting all the blessings of Abraham, Isaac, and Jacob, including "thrones, kingdoms, principalities, and powers, dominions, all heights and depths" (D&C 132:19).

Blessings Promised in the Prophet Joseph Smith's Day

Like Isaiah, the Prophet Joseph Smith, under the inspiration of the Almighty, pronounced great temporal and spiritual blessings and abundance for sincere and single-minded fasting and Sabbath observance. Renewing His Sabbath covenant with the Latter-day Saints in Jackson County, Missouri, in 1831, the Lord declared to Joseph, "Verily I say, that inasmuch as ye do this, the fulness of the earth is yours" (D&C 59:16). This sounds a great deal like riding "on the high places of the earth."

For those early members of the Church who were eking out a living on the untamed American frontier, the Lord assured prosperity and plenty in symbols that would have had great meaning for them: "the beasts of the field and the fowls of the air, and that which climbeth upon the trees and walketh upon the earth; yea, and the herb, and the good things which come of the earth, whether for food or for raiment, or for houses, or for barns, or for orchards, or for gardens, or for vineyards" (D&C 59:16–17).

As these early members sought to build a spiritual as well as a temporal Zion, the spiritual symbolism would not have been lost on them. Everything that the Lord created was for the blessing of His children and also a foretaste of the life they would enjoy one day in His kingdom. He affirms, "Yea, all things which come of the earth, in the season thereof, are made for the benefit and the use of man, both to please the eye and to gladden the heart; Yea, for food and for raiment, for taste and for smell, to strengthen the body and to enliven the soul. And it pleaseth God that he hath given all these things unto man" (vv. 18–20).

Just as we delight in the Lord and His Sabbath, He delights in seeing us delight in the Creation that He hallowed by crowning it with the Sabbath. It all bespeaks of His love, of His fulness that will be ours, of exquisite joy here and hereafter. An implication here is that we should slow down enough in life, at least on the Sabbath, to relish all that He gives us. In fact, Doctrine and Covenants 59 goes on to conclude with a caution that "in nothing doth man offend God, or against none is his wrath kindled, save those who confess not his hand in all things, and obey not his commandments" (v. 21).

Blessings Promised in Our Day

As we pointed out in the preface, the Lord has revealed to the prophets, seers, and revelators who guide the Church that greater blessings await the Saints if they will renew and strengthen their Sabbath devotion. According to Elder M. Russell Ballard, as they sought the Lord's guidance for the best way to spiritually strengthen members of the Church, ensure lasting conversion and covenant keeping, and create multigenerational families faithful to the Church, the answer became clear to them—"keeping" and honoring the Lord's day, the Sabbath.

As we study the blessings enumerated in the scriptures, it is easy to see why that answer was given to the Brethren. "As we learn better how to hallow the Sabbath day," taught President Russell M. Nelson in the same conference, "faith will increase across the world." We believe that as we seek to follow our inspired leaders and demonstrate deeper faith in the Lord Jesus Christ by greater reverence for the Sabbath and the sacrament, we will see these blessings fulfilled in our own lives and in the lives of those we love. The Church will be strengthened and its influence for good will grow. Perhaps even whole nations will be blessed. What blessings await you and your family as you sanctify this day?

As we have noted, the First Presidency and the Twelve did not feel that the Church needed new programs to strengthen it, but rather a refocus on one of the most basic commandments. "We human beings have a strange tendency to complicate simple things," remarked President Dieter F. Uchtdorf in the 2012 Worldwide Leadership Training broadcast. "We set up rules, laws, bylaws, processes, and sub-processes. Eventually, we pile up load after load until we end up under a huge weight of expectations that are so complicated it is difficult to keep track of them, let alone meet them."[41]

Likewise, we can imagine that with this renewed emphasis there will be a temptation to create—or at least feel pressured to create—elaborate activities for our families to participate in on the Sabbath, structuring every moment of the day. Planning activities for yourself and family members that will strengthen them is a good thing. We should have a plan for our Sabbath days, but it should not create pressure or expectations that cause us to dread the Sabbath.

Time for personal quiet, prayer, scripture study, and reflection is important as well as time for some unstructured, no-pressure, just-being-together moments. And while an extra-nice dinner is a great way to set the day apart and give our best, even that should be done with "singleness of heart." This singleness of heart includes a single purpose—to honor the Lord, not to impress others. "And on this day thou shalt do none other thing, only let thy food be prepared with singleness of heart that thy fasting may be perfect, or, in other words, that thy joy may be full" (D&C 59:13).

"Singleness of heart" has more to do with *why* we worship and *how* we worship in our hearts and souls and families, rather than just *what* we do. Simplicity is implied in this passage. But what is simplicity to one family may be "too much" for others. To us,

---

[41] Dieter F. Uchtdorf, "Acting on the Truths of the Gospel of Jesus Christ," *2012 Worldwide Leadership* Training; www.lds.org/broadcasts/article/worldwide-leadership-training/2012/01/acting-on-the-truths-of-the-gospel-of-jesus-christ?lang=eng

"singleness of heart" means that all we do and all we feel is "with an eye single to the glory of God" (see D&C 82:19; 88:67–68).

Outcomes

In keeping our Sabbath observance simple and focused, we believe Elder D. Todd Christofferson had the best idea of all about how to frame our planning for our Sabbath-day worship. During a discussion by a panel of general Church leaders at the October 2015 Leadership Training Meeting, the topic turned to service, including community service, on the Sabbath. While speaking specifically of service being rendered on the Sabbath, Elder Christofferson gave valuable counsel that can guide us as we plan and execute all of our activities on that sacred day:

> To me the key to that [planning our Sabbath activities] is [to] focus on outcomes—what do we want to have happen? what sign do we want to give?—and when we've got that kind of a focus then naturally there comes into play activities of service and other kinds of things that achieve those ends, and we don't have to have lists of dos and don'ts.[42]

This is the focus each individual and family needs. What do you really want to gain from your Sabbath worship? What righteous outcomes do you want your family to experience? Each family and person must adapt according to their needs and circumstances and seek the confirmation of the Spirit. As you do, remember that learning to keep the Lord's day holy is a process and an attitude and not a destination or a perfect performance. Circumstances and people can shift from week to week. This can require great patience with others and ourselves. The Lord knows our motives, appreciates our efforts, and will lead us along.

The beauty of the Lord's commandment to keep the Sabbath day holy is that we get to try again every seven days. It is a process of continually refining our efforts and our attitude and seeing progress and a change in ourselves as we look back over the years. When we

---

[42] D. Todd Christofferson, General Conference Training, October 2015.

are getting it right, the Lord will let us know. We will know by the way we feel about ourselves and about the Lord. He will let us know by the blessings that come into our lives and our families.

When we kneel at our bedside each Sabbath night, we can take inventory of how we did and how we can do better next week. You, like everyone else, will make mistakes—but if every once in a while you feel exquisite joy and gratitude at the end of the Sabbath day, you know you are on the right path. You have progressed from merely refraining from breaking the Sabbath to truly relishing it. You have glimpsed eternal life.

As we seek to sanctify the Sabbath, we are sanctified ourselves. "Sanctifying the Sabbath is part of our imitation of God, but it also becomes a way to find God's presence."[43] What greater blessing can we have than to have God's presence in our hearts and in our homes? Isn't that what the Sabbath is really all about?

---

[43] Heschel, *The Sabbath*, 13.

ABOUT THE AUTHORS

WENDY C. TOP ATTENDED BRIGHAM Young University and is the author of *Getting Past the Labels: How the Truth Makes Women Free*. With her husband, Brent, she coauthored *Glimpses Beyond Death's Door*, *Finding Inward Peace*, and *Finding God in the Garden*.

Sister Top has served in the Church in many leadership and teaching capacities; among them, she served as a full-time missionary with her husband when he presided over the Illinois Peoria Mission from 2004 to 2007. She is the mother of four and the grandmother of sixteen.

BRENT L. TOP IS PROFESSOR of Church history and doctrine at Brigham Young University, where he also serves as dean of Religious Education. He also served for several years as department chair and associate dean.

He has authored and coauthored numerous books, including *Strength through Adversity*; *What's On the Other Side?*; *LDS Beliefs: A Doctrinal Reference* (with Robert L. Millet, Camille Fronk Olson, and Andrew C. Skinner); *When You Can't Do It Alone*; *Beyond Death's Door*; *The Life Before*; and *The Doctrinal Commentary on the Book of Mormon* (with Robert L. Millet and Joseph Fielding McConkie).

He and his wife, Wendy, reside in Pleasant Grove, Utah, where he serves as a stake president.